The Civil Rights Movement

The Civil Rights Movement

AN ILLUSTRATED HISTORY

BRENDA WILKINSON

CRESCENT BOOKS

NEW YORK • AVENEL

Page 1: Aftermath of the fatal shooting of two Jackson State College students in Jackson, Mississippi.

Pages 2–3: The historic March on Washington, August 28, 1963.

This page: Gary, Indiana, high school students boycott "Freedom Day" in city schools on account of de facto segregation.

Acknowledgements

The author would like to thank Betty Thompson for her editorial advice, and the following individuals who provided assistance with research: Peggy Billings; David Briddell; Mary B. Davis; James Haskins; Sharon Howard; William Robinson; Carol Strader; and Chereyetta Williams.

The publisher would like to thank Robin Langley Sommer, senior contributing editor; Julia Banks Rubel, associate editor; Nicola J. Gillies, editorial assistant and indexer; Sara Hunt, photo editor; Gillian Speeth, picture research; Charles Ziga, art director; Christopher Berlingo and Wendy J. Ciaccia, graphic designers. Photographs courtesy of the Prints and Photographs Division, Library of Congress, except those listed below:

© 1996 **Archie Hamilton**: author photograph, jacket flap; **Corbis-Bettmann**: 10, 14, 15, 19, 22, 32, 34, 35, 38, 39t, 40b, 41, 42, 70b, 74, 75, 77b, 79t, 81, 82b, 95br, 135b, 150; **UPI/Corbis-Bettmann**:1, 2–3, 4, 6, 7, 8, 11, 12–13, 27, 37, 52, 55, 57, 63, 69, 70b, 71, 73, 76, 77t, 78, 79b, 80, 82t, 83, 84, 85, 86, 87, 88, 89, 90, 91, 92, 93, 94, 95t & bl, 96, 97, 98, 99, 100, 101, 102, 103, 104–105, 106, 107, 108, 109, 110, 111, 112, 113, 114, 115, 116, 117, 118, 119, 120, 121, 122, 123, 124–125, 126, 127, 128–129, 130, 131, 132, 133, 134, 135t, 136, 137, 138, 139, 140, 141, 143, 144, 145, 146, 147, 148, 149, 150b, 151, 152.

This 1997 edition published by Crescent Books, distributed by
Random House Value Publishing, Inc.
40 Engelhard Avenue
Avenel, New Jersey 07001

Random House
New York • Toronto • London • Sydney • Auckland

Produced by Saraband Inc., PO Box 0032, Rowayton, CT 06853-0032

Copyright © 1997 Saraband Inc.

Design © Ziga Design

A CIP catalog record for this book is available from the Library of Congress

ISBN: 0-517-15963-5

10 9 8 7 6 5 4 3 2 1

Printed in USA

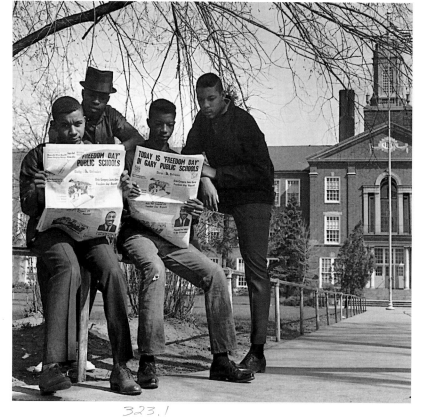

FOR RACHEL HUNT
AND
LULA M. GARRETT

IN LOVING MEMORY

Contents

Introduction

It is simply a fact that black Americans experience discrimination from the cradle to the grave. My own experience with racial prejudice began at my birth.

Born in Moultrie, Georgia, on January 1, 1946, I was the first baby to arrive in the town that year. However, notice of my birth was postponed until a white child came along. Local white merchants, who annually set aside gifts for this occasion, had no intentions of showering a Negro baby, so I was made number two. Such would be my status as I came of age as a colored girl in Georgia during the 1950s.

In a trilogy of novels I wrote in the 1970s, I chronicled what life was like for Southern black children in the fifties. My fictional account contains warmth as well as humor, because despite the degradation of segregation, I, like many young blacks of the pre-Civil Rights period, was nurtured by a family and community of spiritually strong adults. These adults constantly reminded me that being treated as a second-class citizen by no means made it so. I am still sustained and inspired by memories of my family and community, and I write this narrative with reverence for what they accomplished—nurturing and raising self-respecting adults in an often hostile atmosphere and against many odds.

Twenty years removed from my fictional version of growing up Southern, I am less romantic about the past. My idealistic memories have been replaced by a clearer and more mature perspective of the past—I now realize that the fifties were anything but wonderful for colored people.

This was the period when one of the most brutal racial atrocities in the history of this country occurred. Emmett Till, a fourteen-

Opposite: Young demonstrators in Birmingham set out from the 16th Street Baptist Church during the civil rights campaign of May 1963. Most would be arrested within a few city blocks.

Left: Mr. and Mrs. Horace Banker in the wake of an assault on their new home in Folcroft, Pennsylvania, by a white mob that threw rocks and bottles through their windows (August 1963).

Right: A Mississippi signboard points the way to the town of Sumner, where an all-white jury freed the killers of teenage Emmett Till in a five-day trial that made a mockery of the judicial process in 1955.

year-old black boy from Chicago, was murdered in Money, Mississippi, because he said "Bye, baby" to a white woman. Ghastly photographs of young Emmett circulated throughout the black press—photographs featuring a savagely brutalized dead colored boy.

These pictures shocked me more than the first depiction I saw as a child of Africans packed spoon-fashion on a slave ship. I agonized over the images of the Middle Passage because the people packed together so inhumanly were colored like me. But the Till photos evoked even deeper despair because they were contemporary. I couldn't help thinking, *this boy was only fourteen.*

The death of Emmett Till at the hands of grown white men and their subsequent acquittal demonstrated how deep-seated racial hatred was in the South. Prior to leaving Chicago, young Emmett had been warned by his mother about Southern prejudices, but apparently not to the extent that he fully understood the serious implications of her warnings. In an effort to show off in front of his peers, the innocent and naive young

boy dared to speak to the white woman. It was the pathetic need of the woman's husband and friends for revenge of what they saw as a violation of her "white womanhood" that made them brutally murder the boy. This distorted sense of superiority of one group of people over another was a clear indication of the reign of racial hatred and turmoil that would prevail across the South for the next twenty years. With it went an endless list of unjust laws and mindless Southern mores.

Blacks were not allowed to try on clothing in department stores. They could not stay in hotels, eat in restaurants, share common toilet facilities or drinking fountains, or sit in the same section in movie theaters. When sharing common walkways, they were expected to defer automatically to whites. And they were to address them as "ma'am" or "sir" with no such respect in return. Adult black men and women were casually referred to by whites as "boy" or "girl."

These slights were generally accepted without protest by colored people, because they had few choices in a time and place where not only their livelihoods, but apparently their very lives, were in the hands of whites. What could one in need of medical treatment do except enter the side door of a doctor's office if this was required to receive service? However, in those situations where there was a choice, we were admonished by parents and teachers to do without. For example, at the local Dairy Queen in my hometown, Negroes had to purchase ice cream from a side window. It was better to forego the treat of ice cream than to be seen waiting to be served at the colored window, which was only acknowledged after every white person up front had been waited on—no matter who had come first.

As absurd as the idea was of requiring people to buy ice cream from separate windows, there were far more outrageous discriminatory rulings against blacks from the time of their arrival in this country. In an effort to squash possibilities of potential slave uprisings, there was once a ban, again in my home state of Georgia, against blacks playing drums, horns, or any other instrument. This was to deter what had become the official signal among slaves that something of major consequence to them was about to occur.

Whites were relentless in disrupting efforts of blacks to congregate. Religious worship was even banned at times. There were, of course, laws prohibiting the teaching of reading to slaves and free blacks. And again, in an attempt to ward off slave rebellions, there was a law passed in New Orleans in 1817 that forbade them from dancing except on Sundays in a designated area called "Congo Square." Eventually, they were not allowed to dance anywhere in the state. Nor could they purchase medicines and candles, because whites were convinced that these materials were used by Africans to work so-called voodoo magic on them. Another Louisiana law required black women to tie their hair in head scarves and forbade them from wearing jewels, feathers, and other fancy apparel that might attract white men. This was not the first time that dress had been designated for slaves. In 1735 South Carolina required that they wear "Negro cloth," including checked cottons, scotch plaids, and calico. The list goes on, with official decrees not only against slaves, but free blacks, who were not allowed to hold certain positions of employment and denied the right to vote.

It should be noted that while these injustices were most prominent in the South at this time, they were not exclusive to this region of the country. In 1854 Elizabeth Jennings, a black woman in New York, sued the Third Avenue Railroad Company and won financial damages with this ruling: "Colored persons, if sober, well behaved, and free from disease, may ride with whites in New York City horsecars."

It is clear that throughout the history of the United States, discrimination was always present, taking different forms at different times. It has also become clear to me in researching

Left: During the nineteenth century, abolitionists circulated pictures and broadsides that were designed to arouse public sympathy for the victims of slavery. The public became more aware of such conditions as arbitrary punishment, the break-up of families, and the exploitation of black women through these efforts.

Right: The Ku Klux Klan stages a parade in Washington, D.C., on September 17, 1926. The Klan's elaborate hierarchy and regalia are typical of secret societies, which seek to implement their agendas through cult-like trappings that give members a sense of belonging and mission.

some of the details of black history in this country that people fought against slavery and discrimination from the beginning.

In my memory, I can recall how hope for change rose with the Supreme Court decision in *Brown v. Board of Education of Topeka* in 1954, which stated that segregation in schools and other public facilities based on race was unequal. This ruling overturned the 1896 decision in *Plessy v. Ferguson*, stating that separate but equal facilities were constitutional.

Eight years old, in fourth grade at the time of the *Brown* decision, I was too young to understand the significance of this landmark ruling, but I remember how news of it resonated throughout my small community. "It's coming. It's coming," my fourth grade teacher chanted in the back of the classroom to a fellow teacher. As she spoke, her face revealed the combination of joy and fear she felt. Bittersweet, I guess, would best describe her expression—and for that matter, the general mood of blacks across the South. Although there was great anticipation of the possible changes to come, it was widely recognized

that there would be losses as well. My fourth grade teacher, I later learned, was one of the lucky ones who kept her job. Many from the community were not as fortunate. A study by the National Association of Educators in 1972 documented that more than thirty thousand black teachers lost their positions after the *Brown* decision.

Many black-owned businesses were also forced to close. These establishments had once been a way for African Americans to learn a trade in their own community and go on to operate businesses. But they could not survive the competition with the fancy establishments that had been forced to open their doors to blacks. This was a significant loss in small communities, because the number of professional role models for young blacks dwindled. There was a time when African Americans of different economic means lived within the same blocks—that meant that doctors, lawyers, and other professionals lived near middle-class and poorer blacks. While I do not mean to suggest that prosperous people should not have the privilege of living where they choose, there was an advantage to the situation. These professionals, including teachers, were seen by children as "rich" and worthy of high respect—they were adults we wanted to emulate.

Despite such losses, change was desperately needed in the South. Discrimination was the first lesson Negro children got in school, where year after year we received used books, marked-up desks, and other discards from the local white schools. It mattered little to the town leaders that our parents were tax-paying citizens; the inequities were blatant. Black parents supplemented resources in public schools through community and church fundraising efforts. Somehow they found time and means to do this despite the hardworking and low-paying jobs most held.

My mother, a domestic, worked for fifty

Left: Arson was—and is— one of several tactics used by white supremacists to maintain the status quo by frightening dissenters and activists into compliance.

cents an hour, a salary still in place when I reached high school and was hired to perform the very same work after school and on weekends. Through federal funding, my mother, at age forty with eight children, was able to fulfill her lifelong dream of returning to school, where she acquired a nursing degree. Liberation from domestic work would not have come for her in the "old South." Prior to her death, she saw her eldest grandchild, a graduate of Stanford with a master's degree from Princeton, enter a doctoral program at Harvard. Such victory for a Southern black family with humble beginnings like mine is the result of sacrifices by those courageous blacks and whites who struggled for "the cause."

Civil rights legislation brought not only higher education for African Americans, but better housing, jobs—and beyond all this, greater justice and dignity to this country.

At century's end, there appears to be a move afoot to roll back the clock and undo much of the good secured. Conservative politicians wish to return to "state control." As one who hails from a state where then Governor Herman Talmadge of Georgia declared the *Brown* decision "a mere piece of paper," I shudder at the thought. For justice is not likely to be served with social and economic programs being controlled at the local level.

Consider that although the *Brown* decision was handed down in 1954, enforcement did not go into effect until 1964, after the government won the right to sue states that did not comply. Only then did small towns like mine proceed accordingly. I never did get to see what my fourth grade teacher said "was coming," because it was a year after I'd graduated from high school before the schools were integrated in my hometown. And like most small places it was done at a snail's pace, with a sprinkling of black children here and there throughout the town's school system. It took outside pressure to achieve full integration.

Hence, it behooves us to keep black history at the forefront of our memories, to be aware of the past as we look toward the future. Black history is very much American history.

PART I

"My Soul Looks Back"

Congress Discusses Constitutionality While The Smoke Of Human Bodies Darkens The HEAVENS.

Black Roots in America

"The man who suffered the wrong is the man to demand redress—the man struck is the man to cry out."

—FREDERICK DOUGLASS, 1852

The first record of blacks in the English colonies of North America is that of twenty Africans who arrived in Jamestown, Virginia, in 1619 aboard a Dutch ship. According to colonist John Rolfe of Jamestown, seventeen African men and three women were purchased as laborers for the thousand-acre plantation of Sir George Yardley, then governor of Virginia. They were not slaves but indentured servants, who expected to be freed after an agreed-upon period of service, usually seven years. Indentured servitude was the means by which many poor Europeans made their way to these shores, exchanging their passages for labor.

European slave traders were active on the west coast of Africa from the 1400s onward. Some Africans themselves participated in the slave trade, especially local rulers who captured and sold other Africans, or exchanged them for guns, rum, cloth, and other items. However, most African rulers did not cooperate with them. As historian Lerone Bennett cites in *Before the Mayflower*:

Mani Congo, a ruler in the Portuguese colony of the Congo, made a desperate plea to John Paul II of Portugal to assist him in halting the slave trade in 1526. [His message read:] "We need from your kingdom no other than priests and people to teach in schools, and no goods but wine and flour for the holy sacrament. That is why we beg of Your Highness to help and assist in this matter com-manding the factors that they should send here neither merchants nor ware, because it is our will that in these kingdoms of the Congo there should not be any trade in slaves or markets for slaves."

THE SLAVE TRADE

The African ruler's plea fell on deaf ears, as the traffic in human suffering continued and increased. The captives came from nearly every region of the continent, with most of them from west and central Africa: present-day Zaire, Nigeria, Ghana, Senegambia, and Liberia. They included members of the Hausa, Mandingo, Ibo, Efik, Bambara, Ashanti, Dahomean, and Senegalese tribes, and spoke as many languages and dialects.

Opposite: A nineteenth-century engraving showing an abolitionist view of Southern plantation life.

Previous pages: Somber demonstrations march to protest lynching, an evil that the NAACP was instrumental in bringing to public awareness. Washington, D.C., June 1922.

Left: An artist captures the arrival of a Dutch vessel carrying blacks to Jamestown, Virginia, in 1619.

Slaves sold for as little as the equivalent of twenty-five dollars in merchandise: their market value in the New World was about one hundred and fifty dollars.

The long journey of the captives began on foot, with many dying of thirst and hunger en route to the coast. Survivors who made it to the ships were then forced to endure the Middle Passage—the trans-Atlantic voyage—where they were packed together like animals, without sufficient food, clothing, or sanitation. Chilling testimony to life on a slave ship was given by Olaudah Equiano (Gustavus Vassa), a Nigerian born in 1745 and captured at the age of eleven. He recalled his ordeal in 1793 in *The Interesting Narrative of the Life of Gustavus Vassa*:

The first object which saluted my eyes when I arrived on the coast was a slave ship riding at anchor waiting for its cargo. This filled me with astonishment, which was soon converted into terror when I was carried on board. I was immediately handled, and tossed up to see if I were sound, by some of the crew; and was persuaded that I had got into a world of bad spirits; and that

they were going to kill me....I was not long suffered to indulge my grief: I was put down under the decks, and there I received such a salutation in my nostrils as I had never experienced in my life; so that, with the loathsomeness of the stench, and crying together, I became so sick and low that I was not able to eat, nor had I the least desire to taste anything.

In a little time after, amongst the poor chained men, I found some of my own nation, which in a small degree gave me ease of my mind. I inquired of them what was to be done with us? They gave me to understand we were to be carried to these white people's country to work for them. I then was a little revived, and thought, if it were no worse than working, my situation was not so desperate: but still I feared I should be put to death, the white people looked and acted, I thought, in so savage a manner; for I had never seen among any people such a brutal cruelty; and this not only shewn toward us blacks, but also to some of the whites themselves.

The stench of the hole while we were on the coast was so intolerably loathsome, that it was dangerous to remain there for any time, and some of us had been permitted to stay on deck for the fresh

Right: *The monstrous and inhuman conditions of slave ships were justified by their economics: the more slaves transported, the bigger the profit.*

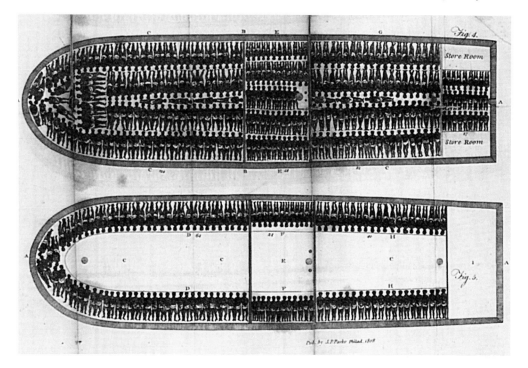

Left: To prevent insurrection and mutiny, insubordinate slaves were often thrown overboard by slave-ship crews.

air; but now that the whole ship's cargo was confined together, it became absolutely pestilential. The closeness of the place, and the heat of the climate, added to the number in the ship, which was so crowded that each had scarcely room to turn himself, almost suffocated us. The shrieks of the women, and the groans of the dying, rendered the whole a scene of horror almost inconceivable.

One day, when we had a smooth sea, and moderate wind, two of my wearied countrymen, who were chained together (I was near them at the time), preferring death to such a life of misery, somehow made through the nettings, and jumped into the sea; immediately, another quite dejected fellow, who, on account of his illness, was suffered to be out of irons, also followed their example; and I believe many more would very soon have done the same, if they had not been prevented by the ship's crew, who were instantly alarmed. Those of us that were the most active were in a moment put down under the deck; and there was such a noise and confusion amongst the people of the ship as I have never heard before, to stop her, and get the boat out to go after the slaves.

However, two of the wretches were drowned, but they got the other, and afterwards flogged him unmercifully, for thus attempting to prefer death to slavery. In this manner we continued to undergo more hardships than I can now relate, hardships inseparable from this accursed trade.

Another description of the slave ship voyage, four to eight weeks in duration, is provided in Charles Christian's *Black Saga*:

Women, men and children were crammed so tightly in the ships that out of a load of seven hundred slaves, three or four would be found dead each morning. Most ships had three decks, the lower two used for transporting slaves. The lowest deck was no more than five feet high. Slaves were packed into it side by side to utilize all available space. In the next deck, wooden planks, like shelves, extended from the sides of the ship, where slaves, chained in pairs, were crammed side by side.... Although buckets were provided for use as toilets, they were not emptied regularly. The ships smelled of excrement, disease, and death.

There are no accurate figures as to how many Africans were brought to this country and others during the four hundred years when the slave trade flourished, but it is estimated that the continent lost more than 15,000,000 of its people and that between 15 and 20 percent of these died en route to the colonies. However, they did not leave their homeland without a struggle, as historian William Loren Katz documents in *Eyewitness: The Negro in American History,* with quotations from Captain Philip Drake, a slave trader for fifty years: "The Negroes fought like wild beasts...Slavery is a dangerous business at sea as well as ashore. A seaman aboard a slave ship wrote in his diary: 'If care not be taken the slaves will mutiny and destroy the ship's crew in hopes to get away. To prevent such misfortunes we visit them daily, narrowly searching every corner between decks, to see whether they have...any pieces of iron, or wood or knives.' "

SANCTION OF SLAVERY

The fact that only three women were among the twenty Africans to step ashore in Jamestown suggests that some of the female captives may not have survived the journey. Of the three who did, Isabella married Anthony and gave birth to William, the first African-American child of record.

The systematic plan of indentured servitude lasted for about forty years in Virginia. Individual blacks continued to work and buy their freedom. A few went on to purchase servants themselves, but in many cases this so-called ownership involved free persons who had purchased their own wives, husbands, children, and other relatives. There were also compassionate purchases of their countrymen by free blacks for the purpose of liberating them from bondage.

During this period, free black men could buy and sell land; they made contracts and enjoyed the same privileges as white colonists.

Right: Upon arrival in the United States, slaves were displayed like livestock and auctioned to the highest bidder, as in this scene from South Carolina. They were often stripped of their clothing to emphasize their health and fitness for labor.

But as more Africans were brought in, the Virginia House of Burgesses passed laws whereby newly arrived Africans and children born to them were defined as slaves who could not become free. This occurred because African labor was proving important to the agricultural economy of colonial Virginia. More than half the original settlers died of malaria in this marshy region. Attempts had been made to use Native Americans as slaves, but they often escaped and returned to their tribes. White indentured servants, too, could escape and lose themselves in the larger society because of their skin color. Africans had no such recourse. Additionally, they were skilled agriculturists and strong workers. Thus, African labor came to be at a premium. As demand for the labor-intensive southern crops of tobacco, sugar cane, indigo, rice, and later, cotton, increased, so did the demand for slaves. In some Southern colonies, slaves outnumbered white settlers by two to one before the Revolutionary War.

In the Northern colonies, the use of slave labor in factories and on small farms proved to be unprofitable. There, black slaves, servants, and free men worked as architects, craftsmen, tailors, stone cutters, shoemakers, spinners, iron workers, and in other skilled capacities. Many Africans arrived with such skills as carving and metalwork: the intricate detailing of some colonial buildings has African origins. They also brought scientific knowledge, especially of native remedies for illness and injury. A slave remembered only as Cesar was widely known for his work with roots and herbs: his cure for poison was published in a Massachusetts magazine in 1792. However, many of the accomplishments of slaves were attributed to their owners.

CHANGES IN BLACK SOCIAL STATUS

Despite the obstacles before them, free blacks and slaves excelled in many facets of colo-

nial life, dispelling the myth that they were an inferior people. "I have found amongst the Negroes as great a variety of talents as amongst a like number of whites," observed an early American member of the Society of Friends (Quakers). This religious body, dedicated to nonviolence, had been instrumental in passing a bill outlawing the slave trade in Great Britain in 1807. Quakers were leaders of the abolitionist movement in America from 1688.

Summarizing the contributions of Northern colonial blacks, Katz lists in *Eyewitness* a number of men who distinguished themselves, including James Forten of Philadelphia, who invented a device that helped control sails. Forten built a sail factory that employed fifty black and white workers and used his wealth to further the abolitionist cause. Thomas L. Jennings of New York invented and patented a process for cleaning clothes. One of his sons became a dentist, another a successful Boston businessman. This family, too, used its wealth to finance the antislavery movement. John Jones,

Above: Slaves worked from dawn until dusk picking cotton on Southern plantations; they were beaten if their day's labor did not meet weight requirements.

quently of the plight of educated blacks who had no arena for their talents.

Black suffering was eloquently expressed in the poetry of Phillis Wheatley, who began to write as a slave in Boston at the age of thirteen. She was widely acclaimed for her lyric verse, first published in England in 1773. Freed five years later, she married free black John Peters. Her poetry moved Benjamin Franklin, who spoke out against slavery before the Revolutionary War and was supported by leaders Noah Webster and John Jay.

Another black writer of influence was Jupiter Hammon, who presented his "Address to the Negroes of the State of New York" in 1787. Later, Samuel Cornish and John Russworm would found the nation's first recorded black newspaper, *Freedom's Journal.* Benjamin Banneker, a free black from Baltimore, Maryland, was a mathematician and astronomer who published scientific almanacs (1792–1806). He came to the attention of Thomas Jefferson, then a member of the Virginia House of Burgesses, and appealed to him to assist in the cause of abolishing slavery. In 1769 Jefferson introduced a bill encouraging the emancipation of slaves to the House of Burgesses, but it would not be passed until 1782.

SLAVE CODES AND INSURRECTIONS

Chattel slavery in America had to be rationalized by the concept that slaves were property, not persons, and that their owners must be protected from violence and rebellion. Thus the slave codes were instituted in the South, beginning in Virginia as early as the seventeenth century. They were often altered and adapted to changing conditions, but they all had certain provisions in common. Any person of Negro blood, whether slave or free, was considered a Negro, irrespective of his skin color. Interracial marriage was prohibited, preventing the formation of family ties

who came to Chicago from North Carolina with $3.50 and became wealthy in the tailoring business, helped repeal "Black Laws" that denied equality to Negroes.

Martin Delaney, an African American who studied medicine and law at Harvard, became internationally recognized as a historian, geographer, and spokesperson for the abolition of slavery. He exhorted blacks to "Make an issue, create an event, and establish a national position for ourselves.... Do some fearless, bold, and adventurous deeds of daring." John Rock of Boston, who served variously as a teacher, dentist, doctor, lawyer, and judge, was a staunch believer that blacks were at the forefront of the battle for change. "This being our country," he declared, "we have made up our minds to remain in it, and to try to make it worth living in." He spoke fre-

between poor indentured whites and blacks. The child of a slave mother and a free father—often the plantation owner—was automatically a slave. Slaves were denied the right to own property, to vote, to assemble, to be educated, to own weapons, or to defend themselves against white aggression of any kind. A Virginia slave code dated 1669 permitted slaveholders to kill a rebellious slave with impunity. Usually, however, the codes were enforced by flogging, branding, and imprisonment to avoid the destruction of valuable property. Along with denial of basic human rights was the deliberate effort to destroy black culture through the prohibition of African religious practices, dances, musical instruments, and languages.

Resistance to this oppression came first in individual acts of rebellion. Many slaves escaped to the woods and formed guerrilla groups called "moroons" and "outlyers." As more organized rebellions began to take place across the South, new slave codes were enacted.

Whites in the South, often outnumbered two to one by slaves, feared insurrection. One Northern visitor to the South wrote to an acquaintance, "I have known times here when not a single planter had a calm night. They never lie down to sleep without a loaded pistol at their sides." During the two centuries before the Civil War, there were more than 250 uprisings involving 10 or more slaves bent on personal freedom. The first large-scale revolt was planned by Gabriel Prosser, a Virginia slave, who massed some 1,100 armed slaves near Richmond in 1800. Slowed down by a storm, Prosser and his band were betrayed by a slave who revealed their plans to his master. Prosser and 34 others were hanged.

Denmark Vesey, a free black artisan of Charleston, South Carolina, organized a rebellion in 1822 that would have involved as many as nine thousand slaves, according to some accounts. An educated man from Santo Domingo, his given name was Telemaque, which fellow Africans shortened first to Telmark and later to Denmark. He spoke English and French and had bought his freedom with the proceeds of a lottery ticket. A carpenter by trade, he was respected by slaves and free blacks alike and spent four years stocking weapons and plotting his rebellion. As in the case of Prosser, Vesey was betrayed by a house slave who wanted protect his master. Of the 139 blacks arrested, Vesey and 36 others were executed, 32 were exiled. Whites were puzzled as to why privileged free blacks would risk their lives and positions for their fellow Africans. They did not understand the black solidarity that made the taste of freedom bitter while brothers and sisters remained enslaved. As he was led to the gallows, Denmark Vesey called for his people to continue the fight for freedom.

Below: *A fugitive slave faces the inevitable consequences of his insubordination.*

BLACKS IN THE AMERICAN REVOLUTION

Despite their lowly status and treatment by colonial governments, blacks were called on to serve in the French and Indian War (1756–63). Known in Europe as the Seven Years' War, it resulted in triumph for Britain over French North America. In an attempt to recover the costs of the Seven Years' War, Britain imposed new taxes on the colonies, one of the many sources of growing unrest that finally erupted in the Revolutionary War (1776–83). By this time, blacks made up nearly 700,000 of the colonial population of some 2,500,000. Approximately 5,000 blacks, slave and freemen, served in the Revolutionary armies.

Crispus Attucks, a runaway slave, was one of the first patriots to die, in the Boston Massacre. Slaves were seduced by both sides to volunteer their services for the promise of freedom. In some instances, this promise was fulfilled; often, it was not. The British frequently took black volunteers to the West Indies, where they were enslaved again, and many colonists simply went back on their word. Despite these risks and the general danger of warfare, slaves served loyally. Among them was "Robert Shortliff," who turned out to be a woman named Deborah Gannett. She served for eighteen months in the Patriot army, disguised as a man, and was rewarded by Massachusetts for heroism.

Initially slaveholders opposed black participation in the Revolutionary War, but once the British began to recruit runaway slaves, George Washington ignored objections to black soldiers. Their perseverance was attested to by a white soldier who served with them: "Had they been unfaithful, or given way before the enemy, all would have been lost. Three times in succession they were attacked, with the most desperate valor and fury, by well disciplined and veteran British troops, and three times did they successfully repel the assault, and thus preserve our army from capture. They fought through the war. They were brave, hardy troops. They helped gain our liberty and independence."

THE CONSTITUTION

One would have thought that the liberty and independence gained by the war would be extended to black Americans in the U.S. Constitution, written in 1787. The noble ideals embodied in the Declaration of Independence of 1776, including the key concept that all men were created equal, with inalienable rights to life, liberty, and the pursuit of happiness, were totally compromised by the Constitution's failure to abolish slavery for political and economic reasons. In fact, it included a provision that prohibited

Below: A political cartoon in which the Declaration of Independence statement that "all men are created equal" is mocked by the Constitution's failure to apply it universally.

Congress from outlawing the importation of slaves until 1808 at the earliest. Nevertheless, several Northern states had provided for the abolition of slavery by gradual means. In 1774 Rhode Island had become the first colony (later state) to prohibit the importation of slaves. During the early 1880s, Pennsylvania, Connecticut, Rhode Island, New York, and Massachusetts abolished slavery entirely within their borders.

The "Three-fifths Compromise" of 1787 had allowed states to count up to three-fifths of their black populations as the basis for representation in the U.S. House of Representatives, which maintained an uneasy balance in Congress between the more populous, industrialized North and the agricultural South.

Unfortunately, the demand for slaves in the South actually increased after Eli Whitney's 1793 invention of the cotton gin, which removed the seeds from cotton at fifty times the rate of a person removing the seeds by hand. Congress did prohibit the importation of slaves after January 1, 1808, but the law was poorly enforced. Two new cotton-growing states, Mississippi and Alabama, joined the Union during the 1810s, and the slave population of these regions increased from 75,000 to 500,000 in the period 1820–40. The price of slaves doubled and tripled. The warnings and exhortations of black spokesmen like David Walker of Boston, who published an appeal in 1820 stating that "America is as much our country as it is yours," were widely ignored and overridden.

Below: Eli Whitney's invention of the cotton gin in 1793 only increased the demand for slaves in the South.

Stirrings of Conscience

"The progress of emancipation is certain. It is certain because God has made of one blood all nations of men."

—Nathaniel Paul, 1827

National ambivalence about the status of black Americans led to many political compromises during the years between the Revolutionary and Civil Wars. The Northern states opposed slavery. They feared that the Southern states would win control of Congress if the western territories were admitted to the Union as slave states. After much debate, Congress passed the Missouri Compromise of 1820. This law provided that Missouri would be admitted as a slave state, but banned slavery in any other new state north of Missouri's southern boundary. An uneasy political truce would prevail until the Mexican War of 1846–8, which brought vast new Southwestern territories under the American flag. War almost broke out between the increasingly polarized North and South before Congress agreed upon the Compromise of 1850. This settled the issue of slavery in the states to be formed from territory won in the Mexican War and set up federal laws for the return of runaway slaves.

AFRICAN COLONIZATION

In 1787 a British abolitionist society established a community of freed blacks in Sierra Leone, West Africa, called Freetown. The settlement became a British colony in 1808. Paul Cuffee, a free black navigator of New Bedford, Massachusetts, engaged in trade with West Africa and used his own funds to send two shiploads of blacks to Sierra Leone for resettlement.

Born in 1759 near Dartmouth, Massachusetts, Cuffee was one of ten children and had no formal education. Orphaned at the age of fourteen, he became a ship's captain and a businessman who made a fortune in overseas trade, which he used to assist his people. In 1780 Cuffee and eight other blacks petitioned the Massachusetts court about taxation without representation and won the right to vote. He and his brother also opened a school for black children after their own were barred from a New Bedford school. After he established relationships in West Africa, Cuffee taught navigation in Sierra Leone and imported African products to Europe and America.

The second colony founded in Africa for free blacks from the United States was Liberia, established on the west coast in 1822 by the white American Colonization Society. Bordered by Sierra Leone, Guinea, and the Ivory Coast, it would become the second-oldest black republic in the world, after Haiti. The first settlers established a town named Monrovia (after President James Monroe) at the mouth of the Mesurado River (now the St. Paul River).

For obvious reasons, increasing numbers of blacks began to view resettlement in Africa as a better option than remaining in America. More than fourteen hundred had settled in Liberia by 1825. On August 27, 1827, they sent the following message to American blacks:

Opposite: Five generations of a slave family, their somber faces testifying to the hardships they endure, gather before a cabin in South Carolina.

Right: Paul Cuffee, a free black navigator, dedicated his life to elevating the condition of his people. Using his freedom and his financial independence, Cuffee worked to resettle, educate, and gain rights for fellow blacks.

PAUL

CAPTAIN

CUFFEE

1812.

The first consideration which caused our voluntary removal to this country, and the object, which we still regard with the deepest concern, is liberty—liberty, in the sober, simple, but complete sense of the word: not a licentious liberty, not a liberty without government...but that liberty of speech, action and conscience, which distinguishes the free enfranchised citizens of a free State. We did not enjoy that freedom in our native country.

Forming a community of our own, in the land of our forefathers; having the commerce, and soil, and resources, of the country at our disposal; we know nothing of that debasing inferiority with which our very colour stamped us in America: there is nothing here to create the feeling on our part—nothing to cherish the feeling of superiority in the minds of foreigners who visit us....The burden is gone from our shoulders; we now breathe and move freely; and know not...the empty name of liberty, which you endeavour to content yourselves with, in a country that is not yours.

Strong though sentiment may have been to leave America after hearing such a moving call, most African Americans remained opposed to resettlement as a solution to their problems. Further, they had taken issue with

the American Colonization Society, the white group that founded Liberia and was initially supported by blacks—until they realized that the group merely wished to exile them.

In response to this, a protest meeting was organized by Richard Allen, the minister who in 1794 had established the Bethel African Methodist Episcopal Church (AME), the first free black church in America, and James Forten, the wealthy black sailmaker and abolitionist. More than three thousand people attended the meeting, held in Philadelphia, where the following resolution was adopted:

Whereas our ancestors (not of choice) were the first successful cultivators of the wilds of America, we their descendants feel ourselves entitled to participate in the blessings of her luxurious soil, which their blood and sweat manured; and that any measure or system of measures, having a tendency to banish us from her bosom, would not only be cruel, but in direct violation of those principles, which have been the boast of the republic.

Resolved: That we view with deep abhorrence the unmerited stigma attempted to be cast upon the reputation of the free people of color, by the promoters of this measure, that they are a dangerous and useless part of the community...

Resolved: that we never will separate ourselves voluntarily from the slave population in this country; they are our brethren by ties of consanguinity, of suffering, and of wrong; and we feel that there is more virtue in suffering privations with them, than fancied advantages for a season.

Forten had been particularly insulted by the American Colonization Society's offer to make him the head of the Liberian colony, as though self-aggrandizement was a price he would accept for abandoning his people. He had long struggled with the question of colonization, and he concluded at first that "Negroes would be better off in Africa or anyplace but America," a sentiment he conveyed to Paul Cuffee during the 1810s. Later, Forten wrote to Cuffee again, telling him of his change of heart. He became a strong opponent of colonization, convincing William Lloyd Garrison, the respected white editor of the leading abolitionist newspaper, the *Liberator*, that removal of blacks from America was not a just and sound course.

THE BLACK CHURCH

Richard Allen, who shared leadership with Forten at the anticolonization forum, came to be a leading spokesperson for African Americans through his association with the black church, which would remain a major force in the civil rights movement. His establishment of the African Methodist Episcopal (AME) church of Philadelphia resulted from disrespectful treatment of blacks at St. George's Methodist Episcopal Church, a white congregation. In 1787 Richard Allen, Absalom Jones, and other black worshippers were pulled from their knees by a white usher as they prayed. The usher told them that they were in an area reserved for whites. They left the congregation, never to return, and each of them eventually led churches in his own right. Allen and Jones worked together for many years, not only for the abolitionist movement, but for the black community in general. During the yellow fever epidemic of 1793, they were tireless in providing help and care for the sick and burial for the dead. Their devotion was attested to by Benjamin Rush, then the nation's most distinguished physician and a prominent abolitionist.

Gradually, black men were trained and licensed by Baptists and Methodists to preach. Despite the legal requirement that black assemblies be supervised by whites, some whites were opposed even to religious gatherings. They continued to harass black worshippers, convinced that any form of assembly constituted an opportunity for

Left: Benjamin Rush, one of the signers of the Declaration of Independence, was a celebrated physician and an eminent abolitionist.

blacks to denounce and work toward the abolition of slavery, or, in the case of slaves, to escape or revolt.

The first black Baptist Church was founded in 1750 in Silver Bluff, South Carolina, and led by slaves George Liele and David George. The First African Baptist Church was founded in Savannah, Georgia, in 1788 by Andrew Bryan, who was converted by George Liele. Slaves were beaten by their owners for attending Bryan's church, and Bryan himself was arrested. Sympathetic whites fought for his release, and Bryan went on to found three more congregations, always under the distrustful gaze of Southern slaveholders.

NEW INSURRECTIONS OF THE 1830S

The Nat Turner Rebellion took place in Southampton County, Virginia, in 1831 and terrified the entire South. A man of deep introspection, Turner said that a vision had inspired his revolt, which began with a band of six fellow slaves. "I heard a loud voice in the heavens," he proclaimed, "and the Spirit instantly appeared to me and said...I should arise and prepare myself, and slay my enemies with their own weapons."

Above: Under the direction of captive Joseph Cinque, the son of an African king, the slave ship Amistad was seized off the Cuban coast in 1839.

Over a three-day period beginning on August 21, Nat Turner recruited some 70 other slaves as he went from plantation to plantation destroying property and killing families. At least 57 whites died before the state patrol and militia were called out to stop the crusade against bondage. At least 40 slaves were killed at Jerusalem, the county seat, on August 24. Turner and 53 others were arrested, of whom he and 16 others were executed. Later, more than 120 slaves in the vicinity were rounded up and tortured or killed in retaliation.

In 1839 captive Joseph Cinque, the son of an African king, mutinied and seized the ship *Amistad*. He spared the lives of two crew members, who tricked him into thinking they were returning to Sierra Leone; instead, the ship ended up off the shore of Montauk, Long Island, where Cinque and his companions were captured and imprisoned. Later, they were exonerated by the U.S. Supreme Court through the defense of former president John Quincy Adams. It was determined that they had been seized as free men and were therefore guilty of no crime in killing their captors.

EDUCATION

Because Nat Turner, leader of the 1831 rebellion, had been educated, slaveholders became relentless in their efforts to ensure that blacks remained ignorant. Stronger laws were passed that made it a criminal act to educate slaves. A Virginia legislature went so far as to declare, "We have closed every avenue by which light might enter their minds. If you could extinguish the capacity to see the light, our work would be completed; they would then be on a level with beasts of the field, and we should be safe."

Even freemen had restrictions on education, in the North as well as the South. Some communities set up separate schools for blacks; in others, such schools operated illegally. John Chavis, a free black in North Carolina, taught whites during the day and blacks at night, for a smaller fee.

Another pioneering black educator was Daniel Payne of South Carolina, who opened

Right: Nat Turner, an educated slave and leader of the Nat Turner Rebellion, strengthened Southern resolve to keep slaves ignorant and uneducated.

a school in 1829 and taught there until the state passed a law against blacks teaching other blacks, whether free or slave. Payne's school had a curriculum of reading, writing, arithmetic, literature, science, chemistry, botany, zoology, astronomy, and geography. Payne taught himself these subjects, as well as Greek, Latin, and French. Initially he taught children by day and adults at night, charging fifty cents per month. At one point he became discouraged by increasing expenses and gave up his mission, but he returned to teaching after a white man told him that the only difference between a master and a slave was superior knowledge. In 1856 Payne founded Wilberforce University in Xenia, Ohio. His dedication made him one of many black educators who prevailed over limited resources and poor facilities to enlighten black children.

A conscientious white woman influenced by the abolitionist movement was Prudence Crandall, a Quaker schoolmistress who operated a girls' academy in Canterbury, Connecticut, in the early 1830s. As a reader of the *Liberator,* she was moved to admit Sarah Harris, the daughter of a black family, to her school. Harassment finally forced her to close, but she reopened in 1833 as a school for "colored" girls only, with young women from twenty well-to-do Eastern black families.

Renewed harassment came in the form of white citizens' refusal to sell Crandall school supplies; denial of medical services to students; dumping of waste from a slaughterhouse on Crandall's porch; shutting her and the students out of church; stoning them; and seizing the girls on the street for outdated vagrancy laws and attempting to whip them. A local politician came up with a provision of state law that prohibited "boarding or instructing any person of color not an inhabitant of the state without prior approval of the town." Crandall argued that this did not apply to incorporated colleges and academies and was arrested for her refusal to comply.

Crandall went on trial. She was convicted after Judge David Daggett instructed the jury that blacks were not citizens of the United States, a statement that would later give judicial precedent for the *Dred Scott* decision.

Eventually, Crandall's school was firebombed. Her case was set aside and she moved to Illinois. Her conviction was not reversed but was erased from the record years later, and she was granted a small pension for the suffering she had endured.

Below: White teachers, like these women in a Virginia Freedmen's Bureau schoolroom, often defied municipal laws and risked imprisonment for educating blacks.

Since the late 1700s, some colleges had admitted black students, including Bowdoin, Oberlin, Franklin, and Rutland Colleges and Harvard University. Lincoln University for black students began operating in Pennsylvania in 1854, closely followed by Ohio's Wilberforce University. Not until the late 1800s would the base for higher education broaden with the founding of Booker T. Washington's Tuskegee Institute, Howard University, Hampton Institute, and Atlanta and Fisk Universities.

GROWTH OF THE ABOLITIONIST MOVEMENT

Religious, ethical, and political concerns led increasing numbers of Northern whites to join black countrymen in their fight for freedom. Prominent among the religious groups were the American Quakers, who formed the first society for the abolition of slavery in 1688. The Pennsylvania Society for Promoting the Abolition of Slavery was established in 1775, on the eve of the American Revolution. However, it was not until the 1830s that the abolitionist movement became a crusade.

In 1831 William Lloyd Garrison, a white editor, began publishing the *Liberator,* a militant Boston newspaper advocating an immediate end to slavery. The paper offered political and social news along with details on discriminatory acts and any support services available to counter them. Free blacks were often jailed for distributing the paper. In 1843 Garrison became president of the American Anti-Slavery Society (of black and white abolitionists) and served until 1865. A man of vision, he also promoted the cause of women's rights, which some say contributed to weakening the antislavery movement.

In the early 1800s, the Quakers and other antislavery groups had established the Underground Railroad, a system by which 75,000 to 100,000 slaves would eventually escape to the Northern states and to Canada, where slavery was a dying institution. (Slavery would be abolished there in 1833.) Blacks and whites risked their lives to help the runaways escape, passing them safely from house to house and church to church.

A moving power in the Underground Railroad was Harriet Tubman, often called "the Moses of her people." Born into slavery in Maryland in 1821, she escaped with two of her brothers who, lacking her courage, turned back in fear. Tubman returned to the South more than nineteen times, bringing out as many as three hundred slaves, including her parents and siblings. Slavemasters offered a $40,000 reward for capture of this most famous conductor of the Underground Railroad. During the Civil War, she served as a scout and spy for the Union Army.

In 1831 a group of black women, under the auspices of the Female Literary Society, organized for "the mental improvement of females." Led by Charlotte Forten, granddaughter of James Forten, the society collected books and leaflets on slavery and studied ways in which they could help the cause of abolition. Because of her family's wealth, Charlotte Forten had attended an affluent mixed school near Boston as a teenager, but it was not a pleasant experience.

Below: An 1849 engraving entitled "The Mysterious Box" depicts a slave being shipped to freedom via the Underground Railroad.

As she recorded in her diary in 1854: "It is hard to go through life meeting contempt with contempt, hatred with hatred, fearing, with too good reason, to love and trust hardly any one whose skin is white—however lovable, attractive and congenial....Let us take courage, never ceasing to work—hoping and believing that, if not for us, for another generation, there is a better, brighter day in store." Later she served as a teacher in South Carolina and married Francis J. Grimke, a minister who was among the founders of the National Association for the Advancement of Colored People (NAACP). Forten and seventeen other women also formed the Philadelphia Female Anti-Slavery Society, with black women holding leadership roles. In addition to emancipation, they were committed to improving conditions for the black community.

Branches of the Female Anti-Slavery Society spread to other regions, as women established local chapters and invited abolitionist leaders like Garrison to speak. In 1836 Garrison was gang-mobbed and dragged through the streets of Boston at rope's end after attending a Female Anti-Slavery Society meeting. Town officials rescued him and

placed him under arrest for his protection.

Prominent among Southern female abolitionists were the Quaker sisters Angelina and Sarah Grimke of South Carolina. Among other documents, they published a strongly worded "Appeal to the Christian Women of the South" and an "Epistle to the Clergy of the Southern States." Some Quakers were displeased with their efforts, declaring their independent course of action "improper" for women. Much of what they wrote was burned by postmasters and otherwise prevented from circulating as "inflammatory" literature.

Married for a time to fellow abolitionist Theodore Weld, whom she later divorced, Angelina differed with the Society of Friends over women's rights. However, her financial independence allowed her to remain influential and make major contributions, all of them financed from her personal fortune. Her father, John F. Grimke, was a justice of South Carolina's highest court who had been educated at Oxford University.

African Americans gave major support to the women's movement, notably in the persons of Sojourner Truth and Frederick Douglass. A former slave, Sojourner Truth (born Isabella Baumfree) was unable to read or write, but she became a major spokesperson for abolition, prison reform, temperance, and women's rights. In 1851 she attended a New York convention where a male speaker suggested that women should not enjoy equal rights because they were physically and mentally inferior. Truth rose to her feet and galvanized the assembly with her address:

Dat man ober dar say dat woman needs to be helped into carriages, and lifed ober ditches, and to hab de best place everwhar. Nobody eber helps me into carriages, ober mud-puddles, or gibs me any best place. And ain't I a woman? Look at me! Look at my arm! I have ploughed, and planted, and gathered into barns, and no man could head

Left: Harriet Tubman, renowned for her work with the Underground Railroad, helped bring as many as three hundred slaves to freedom, earning her the nickname "the Moses of her people."

Right: Evangelist, reformer, and former slave Sojourner Truth travelled across the nation to speak on behalf of abolition, prison reform, temperance, and women's rights.

me! And ain't I a woman? I could work as much and eat as much as a man—when I could get it—and bear de lash as well! And ain't I a woman? I have borne thirteen chilren, an seen 'em mos' all sold off to slavery, and when I cried out with my mother's grief, none but Jesus heard me. And ain't I a woman?

The speech received thunderous applause, as would so many of her protests, as she went about speaking across the nation on behalf of justice until her death in 1883.

Prejudice manifested itself in New York City when black women attempted to join the New York branch of the Anti-Slavery Society. Not only were they barred by white women members, their request to have a black minister address the group was denied on the grounds that it was counter to "correct social mores." However, enlightened white women like Elizabeth Cady Stanton, suffragist and reformer, recognized the strength in the union of oppressed people. She and Quaker Lucretia Mott organized the first national convention on women's rights in Seneca Falls, New York, in 1848, and it was former slave and abolitionist Frederick Douglass whom she asked to address the audience. She drew

an analogy between his condition and her own with the words, "You, like myself, belong to a disfranchised class, and must see that the root of all our social and legal disabilities lies in our deprivation of the right to make laws for ourselves. Will you urge the convention to adopt this protest [the Women's Bill of Rights] against injustice? I have never spoken in public, and cannot defend my own resolutions. I want your help."

Douglass agreed to speak on this occasion, which took place only three years after the publication of his *Narrative of the Life of Frederick Douglass, An American Slave.* He had been born into slavery in Maryland in 1817 as Frederick Augustus Washington Bailey and learned to read and write from his owner's wife. In 1838 he escaped to New York disguised as a sailor, changed his name, and became a speaker for the Massachusetts Anti-Slavery Society. His commanding presence and powerful voice made him one of the nation's greatest orators. In 1847 he founded the antislavery weekly *North Star,* which was published until 1860. His most quoted address, "The Philosophy of a Great American Reform," (1857) said in part:

If there is no struggle there is no progress. Those who profess to favor freedom and yet deprecate agitation, are men who want crops without plowing up the ground....Negroes will be haunted at the North, and held and flogged at the South so long as they submit to those devilish outrages, and make no resistance, either moral or physical. Men many not get all they pay for in this world, but they must certainly pay for all they get. If we ever get free from the oppressions and wrongs heaped upon us, we must pay for their removal. We must do this by labor, by suffering, by sacrifice, and, if needs be, by our lives.

Papers like the *Liberator* continued to publish statistics on the traffic in black men, women, and children, and the license to kill those who attempted to escape. Determined slaves armed themselves for the flight to freedom. One group of teenagers escaped from Maryland on Christmas Eve 1855. Surrounded by slave-catchers, Ann Wood held a double-barreled pistol in one hand and a long knife in the other and dared them to fire. The posse backed down, and the young people made their way to Philadelphia.

Another daring exploit was that of light-skinned Ellen Cract, who escaped with her dark-complexioned husband by posing as a slaveholder, with her husband acting as coach-man. Henry Brown had himself boxed and shipped North to freedom. The white Southerner who assisted Brown was arrested and sent to prison.

Vigilante groups who pursued slave-catchers continued to spread across the north. One group, the Negro Vigilance Committee of Philadelphia, killed two members of a posse in 1851. Lewis Hayden, an escaped slave living in Boston, kept dynamite in his home, which he vowed to use before allowing slave-catchers to capture those he harbored. Writer and abolitionist Martin Delaney declared boldly: "My house is my castle. If any man approaches that house in search of a slave—I care not who he may be, whether constable or sheriff, magistrate or even judge of the Supreme Court…if he crosses the thresh-old of my door, and I do not lay him a life-less corpse at my feet, I hope the grave may refuse my body a resting place."

Throughout the abolitionist movement, whites continued to assist in the cause, risking their places in the community as well as their lives. Unfortunately, the vigorous efforts of those advocating an end to slavery were opposed, often violently, by those determined to see that it continued. A turning point came with the hotly debated Dred Scott Decision of 1857.

THE DRED SCOTT DECISION

The strength of the Missouri Compromise was challenged in 1846 by Dred Scott, born a slave in Virginia, then taken by his owner into the free state of Illinois and the territory that would become the State of Minnesota, where slavery was forbidden. After being returned to the slave state of Missouri, Scott was purchased by John F.A. Sanford, who agreed with him that he could sue for his freedom because he had lived in a free state and territory. They pursued this suit in hopes that it would further the cause of the abolition movement, and the state circuit court ruled in Scott's favor. The ruling was overturned by the state Supreme Court and appeals brought it to the U.S. Supreme Court in 1857 as *Dred Scott v. Sanford.* The court ruled 6–3 that black slaves were to be considered property; that they had no rights of citizenship; and that Congress could not abolish slavery in a U.S. territory. Southern states celebrated the decision (which would be nullified by the 13th and 14th Amendments to the Constitution), while the North expressed outrage. The resulting polarization pushed the nation closer to civil war.

Left: *Dred Scott was immortalized when the Supreme Court ruled against him in* Dred Scott v. Sanford, *declaring that no black had citizenship as defined by the Constitution and that Congress could not abolish slavery in a U.S. territory.*

The Civil War and Reconstruction

"There was one or two things I had a right to, liberty or death. If I could not have one, I would have the other, for no man should take me alive."
—Harriet Tubman, 1869

The South viewed the growth of the abolitionist movement as an economic threat, a major factor in the eventual secession of southern states and the formation of the Confederacy. Southern politicians continued to argue that Congress should reopen the African slave trade.

In 1854 Congress passed the Kansas-Nebraska Act, which left the issue of the extension of slavery into these two territories to their settlers. Kansas was soon rent by conflict between pro- and antislavery factions. Violence disrupted congressional debate on this issue in 1856, when Senator Charles Sumner, a New England abolitionist, was beaten bloody and unconscious in his study by a colleague, Congressman Preston Brooks of South Carolina. Brooks insisted that Sumner had insulted the South the previous day in his speech entitled "Bleeding Kansas." This outrageous action was applauded in Southern papers with such editorial comments as: "Good!— good!!—very good!!! The abolitionists have been suffered to run too long without collars. They must be lashed into submission…If need be, let us have a caning or cowhiding every day."

Dispute over the Kansas-Nebraska Act led to the emergence of the Republican Party, with Congressman Abraham Lincoln of Illinois as one of its leaders. The party's primary goal was to halt the spread of slavery and preserve the Union intact.

THE RAID ON HARPERS FERRY

Individual determination to fight the institution of slavery came from abolitionist John Brown, whom many thought mad because of the boldness of his insurrection. An active abolitionist since 1839, Brown plotted in 1859 to seize the federal arsenal at Harpers Ferry, Virginia. His plan was to set up a base in the Virginia mountains, to be called the Negro Republic, from which to continue the fight to free slaves. Frederick Douglass attempted to dissuade him, warning that the raid would not be successful. Harriet Tubman would have been part of Brown's failed mission had she not been ill when it took place.

Opposite: Soldiers of Company E, the Fourth U.S. Colored Infantry, at Fort Lincoln in 1865, three years after Lincoln allowed blacks to fight for the Union.

Left: John Brown's failed rebellion at Harpers Ferry, Virginia, polarized public opinion on the issue of slavery and helped set the stage for the Civil War.

Right: Frederick Douglass, author of Narrative of the Life of Frederick Douglass, An American Slave, *was one of the most powerful abolitionist advocates.*

I am not terrified by the gallows, which I see staring me in the face, and upon which I am soon to stand and suffer death for doing what George Washington was made a hero for doing...For having lent my aid to a general no less brave and engaged in a cause no less honorable and glorious, I am to suffer death. Washington entered the field to fight for the freedom of the American people—not for the white man alone, but for both black and white. It was a sense of the wrongs which we have suffered that prompted...Captain Brown and his associates to attempt to give freedom to a small number, at least, of those who are now held by cruel and unjust laws, and by no less cruel and unjust men.

Brown went into battle with nineteen men, including his own sons. Five blacks were part of the raid: Lewis Sheridan Leary, Dangerfield Newby, John Anthony Colby, Shields Green, and Osborn Perry Anderson. Leary and Newby were killed, Copeland and Green, hanged for treason; Anderson escaped.

Defeated by Colonel Robert E. Lee and a detachment of marines, Brown and his men faced death courageously. Upon hearing his sentence, Brown stated: "Now, if it is deemed necessary that I should forfeit my life for the furtherance of the ends of justice, and mingle my blood further with the blood of my children and with the blood of millions in this slave country whose rights are disregarded by wicked, cruel and unjust enactment, I say, let it be done." Brown's wife commented, "I have thirteen children, and only four are left. But if I am to see the ruin of my house, I cannot but hope that Providence may bring out of it some benefit for the poor slave." One of the condemned blacks, John Copeland, wrote to his brother before the execution:

Executed on December 2 at 11:15 AM, Brown reportedly looked calm and serene as he was led to the gallows. According to the *Anglo-African Magazine* for December 1959, "As he stepped out of the door, a black woman, with a little child in her arms, stood near his way. He stopped for a moment, stooped over, and with the tenderness of one whose love is as broad as the brotherhood of man, kissed the child affectionately." To a reporter for the *New York Herald*, he said, "I pity the poor in bondage that have none to help them; that is why I am here; not to gratify any personal animosity, revenge or vindictive spirit. You may dispose of me easily, but this question is still to be settled...the Negro question—the end of that is not yet."

THE ABOLITIONISTS GAIN GROUND

Although Brown failed at Harpers Ferry, the raid impacted strongly on the Southern view of the abolitionist movement. Slaveholders saw now just how strong was the determination of those who fought for freedom. They were also witnessing a new boldness in slaves, who were responding to widespread rumors across the South that freedom was near. Southern militiamen began stocking weapons and drilling for possible insurrections.

The South's position had already been weakened by the 1852 publication of *Uncle Tom's Cabin* by Harriet Beecher Stowe. Selling 300,000 copies within a year, the novel depicted the cruelty of slaveowners and overseers and gave detailed descriptions of the daily suffering of slaves. It condemned Southern society and brought new sympathizers to the cause of black liberation.

The election of Abraham Lincoln as president in 1860 left many abolitionists uneasy because he had not been as outspoken against slavery as other candidates. His primary focus in the famous debates with Stephen A. Douglas had been on preventing the extension of slavery into new territories. Many feared that he would not press for emancipation, but Lincoln supporters were quick to remind skeptics that his actions and expressions in Congress had been antislavery in sentiment. He had said that slavery was "hostile to the poor" and had denounced the *Dred Scott* decision of 1857, whereby the Supreme Court ruled that Congress could not exclude slavery from the territories.

Southerners identified Lincoln with a threat to states' rights, perhaps even to the institution of slavery, and geared up for battle.

THE NATION AT WAR

With seven Southern states having seceded by the time President Lincoln was inaugurated in March 1861, he proceeded cautiously in his efforts to maintain the Union. In his inaugural address, he stated that secession was illegal and that he would hold federal possessions in the South. When Confederate forces fired on the federal garrison at Fort Sumter on April 12, 1861, the Civil War had effectively begun.

Frederick Douglass gave his reaction to declaration of the Civil War in the 1861 editorial "Nemesis":

At last our proud Republic is overtaken. Our national sin has found us out . . . and our face is mantled with shame and confusion. No foreign arm is made bare for our chastisement. No distant monarch, offended at our freedom and prosperity, has plotted our destruction; no envious tyrant has prepared for our neck the oppressive yoke. Slavery has done it all. Our enemies are those of our own household. . . . We have hated and persecuted the Negro; we have scourged him out of the temple of justice by the Dred Scott decision; we have shot and hanged his friends at Harpers Ferry; we have enacted laws for his further degradation, and even to expel him from the borders of some of our States; we have joined in the infernal chase to hunt him down like a beast, and fling him in the hell of slavery; we have repealed and trampled upon laws designed to prevent the spread of slavery, and in a thousand ways given our strength, our moral and political influence to increase the power and ascendancy of slavery over all departments of Government; and now, as our reward, slaveholding power comes with sword, gun and cannon to take the life of the nation and overthrow the great American government.

As the war proceeded, Lincoln faced not only the struggle to keep the border states of Delaware, Maryland, Kentucky, and Missouri

Left: Harriet Beecher Stowe, author of Uncle Tom's Cabin, *the novel that won new sympathizers to the abolitionist cause, with her husband.*

in the Union, but to pacify Northerners who did not embrace the idea of a war against slavery. Many Northerners, some of them new immigrants, openly expressed their weariness with the abolitionist movement. Some simply didn't think this was their battle. Yet there was resistance when seventy-five thousand blacks presented themselves for service in the Union army. Lincoln had called for volunteers, but blacks were turned away, and in one instance even told that this was a white man's war that had nothing to do with the Negro.

Not to be dissuaded, one group of Northern black men organized and began drilling daily in preparation for war until disbanded by the police. Blacks in Boston passed a resolution stating, "Our feelings urge us to say to our countrymen that we are ready to stand by and defend our government as equals...to do so with our lives, our fortunes, and our sacred honor, for the sake of freedom and as good citizens; and we ask you to modify your laws, that we may enlist—that full scope may be given to the patriotic feelings burning in the colored man's breast." Just as blacks had been at the forefront of the abolitionist movement, speaking, writing, and giving financial support, now they sought the right to serve in the war for freedom.

Many Southern slaves escaped to the Union lines as Northern armies drove deeper into Southern territory. Initially, there was no official policy in regard to them: commanders simply used their own discretion. On July 9, 1861, the House of Representatives passed a resolution deeming it the duty of federal troops to capture and return fugitive slaves. However, the abolitionists' demand that the government be more protective of slaves resulted in the Confiscation Act of 1861, whereby former slaves could not be returned to their owners in the rebellious states.

As the Union pressed forward and more Southern slaves joined their ranks, commanders made their own rules on how to deal with them. Camps were set up and managed by Union soldiers, who hired out blacks routinely as cooks, construction workers, or other kinds of laborers. Treatment was cruel and unfair, and many blacks died for lack of proper resources of food, clothing, and shelter.

The refusal of the U. S. government to allow blacks to serve in the Union armies finally drew formal criticism from abolitionists. They saw it an act of cruelty to deprive blacks of the opportunity to fight for the freedom of their sisters and brothers. And there was growing resentment by whites, who felt that they should not be fighting the battle alone. Lincoln, believing that arming blacks would anger the border states, did not yield until 1862, when both Northern blacks and fugitive slaves were enlisted.

Thomas Wentworth Higgins commanded the First South Carolina Volunteers, the first official regiment of ex-slaves, and left an account of the courage shown by his troops:

In almost every regiment, black or white, there are a score or two of men who are naturally daring, who really hunger after dangerous adventures, and are happiest when allowed to seek them . . . . certainly I had such, and I remember with delight

Below: A slave family makes the dangerous ride to freedom, fleeing North to safety that was not guaranteed until the Confiscation Act of 1861.

their bearing, their coolness, and their dash. Some of them were Negroes, some mulattos. . . . They were the natural scouts and rangers of the regiment; they had the two-o'clock-in-the-morning courage, which Napoleon thought so rare. . . .

I do not remember ever to have had the slightest difficulty in obtaining volunteers . . . There were more than a hundred men in the ranks who had voluntarily met more dangers in their escape from slavery than any of my young [white] captains had incurred in all their lives . . . . As to the simple general fact of courage and reliability, I think no officer in our camp ever thought of there being any difference between black and white.

When the official Union call for blacks to serve in the war went out, Frederick Douglass and his two sons were among the first to volunteer. As a soldier, Douglass continued to urge the government to be of greater assis-

Above: Civil War refugees ford the Rappahannock River in August 1862, as troops advance through Virginia.

Left: The first African-American soldiers enlisted in the Union armies were often assigned camp duties as orderlies and cooks.

Right: A poster featuring slavecatchers pursuing a fugitive slave served as warning to others in the South.

Right: A poster featuring slavecatchers pursuing a fugitive slave served as warning to others in the South.

tance to runaway slaves. Meanwhile, prejudice against blacks grew in the North among those growing weary of war. Propaganda was published by Northern papers, including stories of the rape of white women by black men and of abolitionists encouraging miscegenation. Lincoln was charged with having gotten the nation into a war for "undeserving Negroes at the expense of Whites."

Resentment came primarily from the poor and ignorant and was economically based. There were numerous incidents of violence against blacks by whites, generated most often by competition for work. Negro women and children were mobbed in a New York tobacco factory in 1862, and right-to-work fights erupted between blacks and whites in Chicago, Detroit, Cleveland, New Jersey, and

Right: A black regiment of Union soldiers at Camp William Penn in Philadelphia, Pennsylvania.

Boston. In 1863 striking longshoremen were replaced by Negro workers protected by police. The government then began drafting the unemployed white workers, which sent them into a rage. Major riots broke out.

THE DAY OF JUBILEE

Moving closer to emancipation, President Lincoln recommended in 1862 that slaves in the District of Columbia be freed, with financial compensation to owners, and that one hundred thousand dollars be allotted for resettlement of blacks in Haiti and Liberia. He organized a meeting of free blacks and asked them to support colonization. "Your race," he told them, "suffer greatly, many of them, by living among us, while ours suffered from your presence. In a word, we suffer on each side." In June 1862 President Lincoln signed the bill abolishing slavery in U.S. territories. In July it became law that slaves who escaped to Union lines were free.

Finally, on January 1, 1863, came the Emancipation Proclamation, which declared that "all persons held as slaves within any State, or designated part of a State, the people whereof shall then be in rebellion against the United States, shall be then, thenceforward and forever free." Lincoln issued the proclamation "as a fit and necessary war measure," and it freed slaves only in those territories still in rebellion.

By the end of the war more than two hundred thousand blacks had served, some ninety-three thousand of them from Confederate states. Southern troops regarded these soldiers as escaped slaves, and they faced execution if captured. One year after emancipation, Lincoln would write: "Negro troops heroically vindicated their manhood on the battlefield."

Historian William L. Katz writes in *Eyewitness* that the contribution of black troops was remarkable in light of the disadvantages under which they served: "They were placed in segregated units under white officers who were often prejudiced.... Negro regiments were sent into battle with less training than the white regiments...and with inferior weapons. Their medical facilities were worse and their doctors fewer. They suffered greater casualties than whites...The worst hazard was capture by Confederates. Some were sold into slavery, others put to death."

Emancipation was celebrated in the South with shouts of jubilee and prayer: now slave-owners were fleeing instead of Southern blacks. Edmund Ruffin, the Virginia slave-holder who had fired the first shot at Fort Sumter and reported that "I was highly gratified by the compliment and delighted to perform the service," placed his gun to his head and committed suicide. Thomas Wentworth Higgins, the white commander who wrote so eloquently of the bravery of his Negro troops, spoke with equal passion of the Day of Jubilee:

> *The very moment the speaker had ceased, and just as I took and waved the flag, which now for the first time meant anything to these poor people, there suddenly arose, close behind the platform, a strong*

Left: A Union infantryman sits for his portrait by a Civil War camp photographer.

Above: African-American Union soldiers struggled against injustice within the army as well as fighting the Confederates. The April 1865 Confederate surrender meant that the later battle, at least was won.

male voice...into which two women's voices instantly blended, singing, as if by an impulse that could no more be repressed than the morning note of the song-sparrow,

> My Country, 'tis of thee,
> Sweet land of liberty,
> Of thee I sing...

...Firmly and irrepressibly the quavering voices sang on, verse after verse; others of the colored people joined in; some Whites on the platform began, but I motioned them to silence. I never saw anything so electric; it made all other words cheap; it seemed the choked voice of a race at last unloosed. Nothing could be more wonderfully unconscious; art could not have dreamed of a tribute to the day of jubilee that should be so affecting; history will not believe it...the life of the whole day was in those unknown people's song.

THE FREEDMEN'S BUREAU

Officially, slavery ended with the passage of the Thirteenth Amendment to the Constitution on December 18, 1865, but the social, political, and economic justice that blacks had anticipated was not forthcoming.

President Lincoln had proclaimed freedom but had not defined it. No guidelines were given as to how the former slaves were to go about building new lives. What was to come of four million newly freed blacks? Where were they to live? To work? How were they to be educated? The government attempted to answer these questions by creating The Freedmen's Bureau of Refugees and Abandoned Lands.

The first national welfare system, the Freedmen's Bureau was established on March 3, 1865, under direction of the War Department with its primary leadership from former military officers. General Oliver Howard (for whom Howard University would be named) was appointed commissioner. He described the absolute chaos of the time:

In every state many thousands were found without employment, without homes, without means of subsistence, crowding into town and about military posts, where they hoped to find protection and supplies. The sudden collapse of the rebellion, making emancipation an actual, universal fact, was like an earthquake. It shook and shattered the whole previously existing social system. It broke up the old industries and threatened a reign of anarchy. Even well-disposed and humane landowners were at a loss what to do, or how to begin the work of reorganizing society and rebuilding their ruined fortunes.

Faced with an economy devastated by war, blacks and whites were forced into debt as they struggled to raise cash crops. Many former slaves hired themselves out as sharecroppers, trusting in vain that they would be paid fairly for their labor.

The Bureau served not only former slaves, but many poor whites. Millions of dollars were spent on jobs, education, and medical treatment, not always to good effect.

Commissioner Howard was given discretionary authority for disbursement of the allotted funds. Although handicapped by Southern prejudice, the Freedmen's Bureau sustained many lives and made great accomplishments. In its five years of existence, the Bureau fed more than twenty million, resettled more than thirty thousand, opened over fifty hospitals, and spent more than five million dollars on some four thousand schools and colleges, including Atlanta University, Fisk University, Howard University, and Hampton Institute. W.E.B. Du Bois, black scholar, historian, and civil-rights advocate, summarized the Bureau's work in 1903 with the words: "This Bureau set going a system of free labor, established a beginning of peasant proprietorship, secured the recognition

Below: A contemporary depiction of the Emancipation Proclamation being read by a Union soldier to a family of slaves.

Above: Outside the House of Representatives supporters of the first Civil Rights Bill, of 1866, celebrate its passage.

Right: W.E.B. Du Bois, author and civil-rights leader, summarized the pros and cons of the Freedmen's Bureau, the first national welfare system.

of black freedmen before the courts of law, and founded the free common school in the South. On the other hand, it failed to begin the establishment of good-will between ex-masters and freedmen, to guard its work wholly from paternalistic methods which discouraged self-reliance, and to carry out to any considerable extent its implied promises to furnish the freedmen with land."

STRUGGLING FOR LEARNING AND LAND

When the Freedmen's Bureau lost federal support, the American Missionary Society, an interdenominational group, took over with substantial Baptist and Methodist participation. Missionary teachers traveled from the North to help educate former slaves; 45 percent of them were women. Among the black teachers was Charlotte Forten, who had taken part in the abolitionist movement with her parents and grandparents.

Virginia Union, Morehouse, and Spellman Colleges were established by the philanthropic efforts of whites, who found a deep desire among former slaves for education. Children, parents, and grandparents were taught together, with church buildings serving as schoolhouses day and night. A white Tennessee official of the Freedmen's Bureau wrote in 1866 that "the Colored people are far more zealous in the cause of education than the Whites. They will starve themselves and go without clothes in order to send their children to school." Three years later M.A. Parker, a black teacher, observed, "It is surprising to me to see the amount of

Left: *Artist Thomas Nast published this engraving in* Harper's Weekly *in 1867 to dramatize the plight of blacks ostensibly freed during and after the Civil War.*

suffering which many of the people endure for the sake of sending their children to school. Men get very low wages here . . . and a great many men cannot get work at all. The women take in sewing and washing, go out by day to scour, etc."

Southern whites, fearing an increasingly learned black populace, began to target schools and churches with harassment, despite the fact that so much of the welfare effort was directed toward white relief. One Bureau worker in the South reported, "We have fed with government charity rations sixty-four Whites to one colored person."

The government was also giving millions of acres of land to white settlers as the Western frontier opened. Many former slaves hoped for the "forty acres" that Republican congressman Thaddeus Stevens had proposed as their due. Often, they leased property with the understanding that they would eventually be able to purchase it, but found themselves having to return the land to its former owners once the Confederate aristocracy was pardoned by President Andrew Johnson and given sanction to reclaim it. The black sense of entitlement to the land was passionately expressed by former slave Baily Wyat: "We has a right to the land where we are located. For why? I tell you. Our wives, our children, our husbands has been sold over and over to purchase the land . . . And then didn't we clear the land, and raise the crops? And then didn't them large cities in the North grow up on the cotton, on the sugar, on the rice that we made? I say they grown rich and my people is poor."

POLITICAL MILESTONES

The Thirteenth Amendment, which abolished slavery; the Fourteenth Amendment, which secured for blacks the social and civil privileges extended to whites, including the right to make contracts, to own property, and to testify in court; and the Fifteenth Amendment, which guaranteed the right to vote, were all steps toward establishing equality. The latter two amendments were largely ignored after the government withdrew its support from the Reconstruction South, but they would form the infrastructure for the Civil Rights movement of the 1960s.

Right: Newly freed slaves of the Reconstruction era face an uncertain future in a region devastated by the Civil War.

The Fourteenth Amendment passed over the veto of President Johnson, a former slaveowner from Tennessee who had promised blacks that he would be their Moses. He also claimed to disdain the Confederate aristocracy but declared later that "This is a country for white men and, by God, so long as I am President, it shall be a government for white men." His position set the tone for the establishment across the South of Black Codes that were not far removed from fugitive slave laws. These laws tried to regulate black labor and restricted the rights of blacks to bear arms, serve on juries, or attend schools with whites.

Radical Republicans in Congress became a majority in 1866 and passed the Reconstruction Act of 1867, again over the presidential veto. The act divided the two unreconstructed Confederate states (only Tennessee had rejoined the Union by ratifying the 14th Amendment) into five military districts commanded by major generals. Elections were held for new state constitutional conventions providing for black suffrage; some seven hundred thousand blacks registered to vote. In 1868 the Radical Republicans attempted to impeach President Johnson for contempt of Congress and failure to reinforce the Reconstruction Acts. The measure failed by a single vote.

The first staged "ride-ins" by African Americans took place in Charleston, South Carolina, where they gained the right to ride the streetcars. Their victory inspired blacks in Virginia to stage a similar protest. Opposition to these courageous acts by former slaves increased among southern whites, who attacked the black community on three vital fronts: education, voting rights, and religion in the form of independent black churches.

The Ku-Klux Klan, most notorious of the hate groups, was organized in Pulaski, Tennessee, on December 24, 1865. Civil War general Nathan Bedford Forrest and six of his former colleagues founded the KKK to fight Reconstruction through harassment, intimidation, and murder, wearing robes and hoods to disguise their identities. Over time, they became bolder, with many sympathizers publicly acknowledging their affiliation with the Klan or the similar pressure group, the Knights of the White Camellia.

Once blacks won the right to vote, many were elected to political office, although most positions were still held by Southern white

men and Northerners who had come South for personal wealth and aggrandizement. The term "Carpetbaggers" was given to Northerners who moved South with only a satchel to take advantage of the chaotic situation there; "Scalawags" were the Southerners who cooperated with them. Many became wealthy in this period when corruption was rife.

Much has been written about the ignorance and incompetence of black politicians of this era, but a closer look reveals that most were educated, and some had been businessmen before emancipation. Republican presidential candidate James G. Blaine, who served with many of these men during the 1870s, said: "The Colored men who took seats in both the Senate and the House

Left: The establishment of Black Codes throughout the South made African Americans question the true extent of their freedom.

Right: *An Alabama lynching victim whose violent death was memorialized by a photograph inscribed "George Meadows, murderer and rapist, lynched on the scene of his last crime."*

did not appear ignorant or helpless. They were as a rule studious, earnest, ambitious men whose public conduct...would be honorable to any race." Notable among those who served during Reconstruction were Robert Brown Elliott, Congressman from South Carolina; Blanche K. Bruce, the first black to serve a full term in the U.S. Senate; and P.B.S. Pinchback, who served briefly as governor of Louisiana.

Hopes for further progress toward equality were suddenly dashed by the Compromise of 1877. Republican president Rutherford B. Hayes and Democrat Samuel J. Tilden both claimed victory in the presidential election. Tilden won the popular vote, but was one short of a majority in the electoral college. Southern Democrats agreed to support Tilden in exchange for his removal of federal troops and nonenforcement of Reconstruction policies in the South. After the troops were recalled, white supremacy reigned once more, and the country has never recovered. From the 1800s through the 1930s, more than four thousand blacks were lynched in the South. For fifty years, Southern senators succeeded in blocking antilynching legislation.

In their sense of hopelessness, American blacks turned their thoughts again toward emigration to Africa. A leader in this movement was Henry Turner, an African Methodist Episcopal clergyman, who was elected to the Georgia legislature in 1867 and then denied his seat along with other black legislators. He wrote numerous articles advocating emigration, both before and after his departure for Sierra Leone and Liberia: "For the Negro as a whole, I see nothing here for him to aspire after. He can return to Africa, especially to Liberia where a Negro government is already in existence, and learn the elements of civilization in fact; for human life is there sacred and no man is deprived of it, or any other thing that involves manhood,

without due process of law. So my decision is that there is nothing in the United States for the Negro to learn or try to attain to."

Black migration to the "promised land" of the North accelerated as conditions worsened in the South. Endless rules and regulations were implemented. In addition to racial separation in public transportation, hospitals, prisons, schools, even cemeteries, Mobile, Alabama., imposed a 10 PM curfew for blacks. Birmingham, Alabama, forbade blacks and whites to play checkers together. Among the "crimes" that blacks were charged with across the South were seeking another job, using offensive language (not saying "Mister" to whites), and disputing the price of produce. Some were lynched for these so-called offenses, others imprisoned. Historian Lerone Bennett quotes sociologist Fletcher Green, who concluded after a study of Southern chain gangs that he "knew of no parallel except in the persecutions of the Middle Ages and the concentration camps of Nazi Germany." However, on migrating North in their search for a better life, blacks discovered that discrimination was not exclusive to the South, even though work opportunities and salaries were comparatively better.

Skilled jobs for blacks had decreased drastically in the postwar South. Prior to the Civil War, blacks held 100,000 of the estimated 120,000 positions as artisans. But as the number of skilled white workers increased, unions that excluded blacks were organized. When they were permitted to work in the skilled positions, blacks were paid lower salaries. In time, certain jobs were labeled "Negro jobs" and others "White men's jobs" or "clean work." Author Toni Morrison, in her fictional account of a black man who travels North, captures the joy experienced by blacks arriving in New York to discover that many "clean" jobs are open to them. Her character writes home to exclaim that they have all kinds of good jobs in the city—one where they actually pay a person to stand outside a building and simply watch! But although some blacks who migrated North prospered financially, few discovered good living conditions. They were confined mainly to overcrowded apartments in the designated urban pockets that came to be called ghettos.

Others sought their fortune in the West, as with the major exodus to Kansas organized by Benjamin "Pap" Singleton.

EROSION OF THE FOURTEENTH AMENDMENT

The 1873 Supreme Court ruling in the "Slaughterhouse" cases declared two categories of citizenship—state and federal. As a health measure, the State of Louisiana had chartered a meat-packing company and given it a monopoly. A group of white butchers claimed that this violated the Fourteenth Amendment by depriving them of life, liberty, or property without due process. The court ruled that "the Fourteenth Amendment protects **federal** [emphasis added] civil rights, not the civil rights heretofore belonging exclusively to the states." This action resulted in numerous rulings that denied blacks equal access in hotels, railroads, and other public accommodations. Essentially, the court said that the Fourteenth Amendment forbade states to discriminate, not individuals, thereby giving rise to "Jim Crow," a phrase that dates back to 1830, when Thomas Rice, a white entertainer, observed a black singer-dancer performing in an alley. He "borrowed" the man's dance routine, costume, and song for his own performance: "Wheel about, turn about, dance, jest so—every time I wheel about I shout Jim Crow!" The character became a source of amusement to whites and scorn to blacks.

The North had de facto segregation by way of discrimination in housing, employment, access to public facilities, and other aspects of daily living, while the South had "legal" racial separation and discrimination via what came to be known as "Jim Crow Laws." Tennessee passed the first such law in 1875, declaring segregation in public transportation. It also passed two laws that came close to returning blacks to slavery: the Contract Labor Law, which prohibited anyone from encouraging a laborer to break a work contract; and the Vagrancy Law, which made it unlawful for an individual to be without visible means of support. These two work-related laws were passed to ensure an endless supply of cheap or free labor. Blacks were randomly picked up on vagrancy charges, then "hired" by the state to work off their jail debts.

Along with vagrancy fines being paid off through unpaid work, without pay, numerous other harassment tactics were applied. Propaganda was spread about the difficulty blacks who traveled North experienced, and attempts were sometimes made actually to block safe passage of those attempting to leave the South. Stories are told of blacks stealing away North in the night as if they were still part of the Underground Railroad of slavery days. Southern politicians brought frivolous conspiracy charges against their Northern counterparts in Congress, whom they alleged were attempting to gain political power by bringing blacks North.

Following Tennessee's lead, other Southern states passed Jim Crow Laws. In 1892 Homer Plessy challenged Louisiana's railroad segregation law. The railroad company, which found maintaining separate cars too expensive, encouraged Plessy's lawsuit, in which he protested his arrest for sitting in a coach designated for whites only. Plessy lost the case, which went all the way to the Supreme Court. The Court ruled eight to one that the 14th Amendment allows "separate but equal" accommodations.

The Plessy decision not only set back social progress, but was detrimental to the economy. Segregated schools, hospital wards, even jails were required in the South. The cost of maintaining these separate facilities made for inferior services for all involved. The greater tragedy, however, was that those who sat on the highest court in the land had no vision of racial unity and true equality. Ordinary citizens like one Alabama planter of the period could comment, "If we cannot whip the Negro, they and I cannot live in the same Country." And a Southern newspaper would dare to editorialize: "There must be a mudsill to society...In the South that mudsill is the Negro. They are free, and let them continue free—but let them be **free Negroes.** One [race] must be superior, one must be dominant." Contempt for blacks was such that three Southern senators of the period would demand their deportation, and Wilkinson Call of Florida would propose that America pay Spain fifty million dollars

Below: With few opportunities for employment, blacks were often forced to join labor gangs to survive.

for Cuba to be used as a place to resettle African Americans.

Having shattered dreams of social and economic progress, Southern state governments enacted measures to ensure that blacks would not be part of the political process. They were declared ineligible to vote on grounds that they were illiterate, that they were not substantial property owners, and that they were not descendants of persons who had voted prior to 1866. The latter measure was called the "grandfather clause" because it allowed all whites to vote if their grandfathers had voted, whereas no black who had been enslaved could be enfranchised. Mississippi was the first state to establish the Grandfather Clause, in 1890; South Carolina followed in 1895 and Louisiana in 1897. North Carolina, Virginia, Alabama, Georgia, and Oklahoma followed with additional laws to disenfranchise blacks.

Without protection from the law, lynchings of African Americans escalated. Peonage became the new form of slavery, as helpless blacks became trapped in an endless rent-and-credit system. The Supreme Court declared peonage unlawful in 1911, but the ruling was simply ignored in Southern districts.

Taxation without representation, lack of security for their lives and property, and the daily insults endured by blacks increased migration to the North. Many were now educated, but had to compete with growing numbers of European immigrants for jobs. Throughout the North, many former businessmen worked in menial jobs as porters and common laborers.

The election of Democrat Grover Cleveland as president in 1884 strengthened reactionary forces and began the decline of Republican power. With Republican advocates for civil rights succumbing to the new political majority, the plight of African Americans received even lower priority. Black journalists like the influential editor Thomas Fortune continued to report the atrocities occurring in the South, but their protests were countered by Southern propaganda that blamed lynchings on alleged black crimes. As the North moved still further into industrialization, its press fell silent for fear of antagonizing business interests. Individual spokespersons like Lloyd Garrison and Thomas Higginson, former advocates for blacks, had grown complacent: Higginson went so far as to lecture on blacks' lack of qualification for civil and political rights.

Throughout this period, Frederick Douglass, the leading African-American voice, no doubt weary from so many years in the struggle, is said to have been "erratic," supporting and then opposing emigration. But his militant spirit revived before his death in 1895, when he denounced the country for betraying the freedmen and the Constitution. Douglass's marriage to a white woman was not uncommon for black men of his time and stature. According to historian Carter Woodsen, "Just after emancipation, Negroes were looked upon as the 'coming people.' Thousands were working for their uplift through the church and school. They could vote and hold office. More industrious, too, than the poor whites…[they] often became the more progressive element in the community. Prosperous Negro men, therefore, sometimes seemed more attractive to white women than males of their own race." However, fear of intermarriage or miscegenation would become central to the Southern attack on social equality. Federal laws that allowed the races to mingle in schools and other public places would inevitably lead to mixed marriages: Southern demagogues declared that if such laws meant that they were unable to protect "white womanhood," then the law could be damned.

Hope Deferred Again

"The Spirit calls me. I must go."

—Sojourner Truth, 1877

After the death of Frederick Douglass in 1895, Booker T. Washington became the leading spokesperson for African Americans. Born Booker Taliaferro in Virginia in 1856, he was raised in a poor family. He worked in the salt and coal mines while attending school at night. Determined to continue his education, he walked and hitch-hiked to make the three-hundred-mile trip from his home to Hampton Normal and Agricultural Institute. There he offered to do janitorial work in exchange for his tuition and was accepted as a student. The headmaster of the school secured additional financial assistance for him.

BOOKER T. WASHINGTON

Successful in his studies, Booker T. Washington eventually taught at Hampton and later studied at Wayland Seminary in Washington, D.C., where he took his surname. Returning to Hampton at the request of General Samuel Armstrong, he established a program for American Indian students, using a model he would be asked to adapt for blacks at Tuskegee, Alabama, where he organized the Tuskegee Institute for vocational and professional training. He opened Tuskegee on July 4, 1881, with thirty students in a one-room church. Later he purchased a hundred-acre farm for the practice of agriculture, the major course of study.

Students at Tuskegee not only raised and processed their own food, but designed and built the first structure on the campus. Poor blacks contributed to the institute through donations of food, livestock, and small amounts of money. Major funding came from the Rockefeller and Carnegie Foundations, which were impressed with the agricultural progress emanating from what came to be known as the "Tuskegee Machine."

George Washington Carver, one of the most famous members of Tuskegee's faculty, experimented with agricultural production and chemical derivatives from crops. The son of slaves, he became a leading botanist in crop rotation, developing hundreds of uses for peanuts and sweet potatoes, two inexpensive staples of the Southern diet. He attended Simpson College in Indianola, Iowa, and became the first African American to be admitted to Iowa State College, where he graduated at the top of his class. Carver worked as an agricultural assistant at Iowa State while he studied for his master's degree. During his tenure at Tuskegee, he was asked by inventor Thomas A. Edison to join him in his scientific work in Menlo Park, New Jersey, but Carver declined: he preferred to stay where he was to help impoverished Southern farmers. At his death in 1943, George Washington Carver left his life's savings, some $60,000, to establish a research foundation at Tuskegee.

A renowned speaker, Booker T. Washington organized many conferences to address the problems of farmers. Progressive whites like Henry C. Grady, editor of the *Atlanta Constitution*, began to cooperate in spreading

Opposite: Arrested and beaten during the 1944 Harlem riots, this African American is the victim of an all-too-common experience for black Americans—police brutality.

the news of his work. In 1895 supporters like Grady organized the Cotton States and International Exposition in Atlanta, Georgia, which drew approximately eight hundred thousand visitors. They invited Washington to join them in their successful appeal to Congress for funding, and he was named consultant on black concerns. Speaking at the exposition's opening, he gave an address that would become the subject of much debate in the black community. The strongest dissenter was W.E.B. Du Bois, then emerging as a strong voice in black American affairs. His formal education had begun at Fisk University and ended with a Ph.D. from Harvard (1895). He would begin teaching at Atlanta University in 1897.

Du Bois and other critics dubbed Booker T. Washington's speech "The Atlanta Compromise" because of his statement that "In all things that are purely social [blacks and whites] can be as separate as the fingers, yet one as the hand in all things essential to mutual progress." This was interpreted by Du Bois and like-minded critics as ensuring the continuance of segregation. Du Bois' criticism was explicated in his book *The Ways of White Folks*. The essay entitled "Of Booker T. Washington and Others" charges that Washington asked black people to give up political power; insistence on civil rights, and higher education for Negro youth.

Washington, on the other hand, foresaw the political and economic future of blacks in the South. Witnessing their mass exodus to the North, where de facto segregation prevailed, he advised: "Cast down your buckets where you are." He had grown up and received his education under difficult circumstances, and his world view differed from that of the average educated African American of this era. Proficient on the farm and in the classroom, he recognized that an economic base was key to the improvement of black living conditions. Hence, he concentrated on developing the areas where most blacks were then employed—agriculture and various trades. He believed that African Americans should try to gain economic independence before civil rights. Carter Woodsen observes, "He insisted that since the Negroes had to toil, they should be taught to toil skillfully. He did not openly attack higher education for Negroes, but insisted that in getting an education they should be sure to get some of that which they can use." In fact, the key issue in the Du Bois–Washington debate was how blacks could most effectively improve their situation—in mainstream society, or outside it.

However, Washington's critics heard something different. They accused him of compromising the free choices of black people and paving the way to a future of perpetual servitude. They were also concerned about his hesitancy to attack the Jim Crow laws enacted after Reconstruction, which had perpetuated Southern black poverty

Right: Booker T. Washington, a leading spokesperson for civil rights, was instrumental in furthering the cause of black education. Countless schools were named for him during the twentieth century.

Opposite: The Ku Klux Klan has terrorized African Americans and equal rights sympathizers with the burning cross, a warning of future assaults, since 1866. Disguised in white robes and masks, Klan members use fear and violence in their drive for white supremacy.

through the system of sharecropping, institutionalized segregation, and one-party (Democratic) politics.

History shows that the theories of both Washington and Du Bois had wisdom and validity. It was neither practical nor possible for everyone to pursue the life of an intellectual. On the other hand, vocational students needed instruction from black scholars with academic backgrounds. Some historians, including Lerone Bennett, suggest that the debate between Du Bois and Washington was not so much about academic versus vocational education as it was about leadership. Du Bois opposed Washington's exclusive stress on education of the hand and heart, because without a "knowledge of modern culture" black Americans would have "to accept white leadership, and...such leadership could not always be trusted to guide the Negro group into self-realization and to its highest cultural possibilities."

The debate continued and still does, but Washington's voice reigned supreme for the day. His philosophy was applauded by Southern whites and Northerners alike, who took comfort in the development of a "lower" class of laborers. After his 1895 speech in Atlanta, honorary degrees were conferred upon Washington by Harvard and Dartmouth, and philanthropists donated millions to his programs. The Carnegie Foundation established a personal fund for his discretionary use. His moving autobiography, *Up From Slavery* (1901), was a best seller.

In 1900 Washington organized the National Negro Business League. His control and influence over black affairs was little short of a monarchy, with leading whites as high as the president seeking his counsel and opinions. Few black leaders dared speak out against him because of the political influence he wielded. Careers could be made or broken by this man.

W.E.B. DU BOIS AND THE NAACP

At the age of twenty-six, the brilliant Du Bois accepted a teaching job at Ohio's Wilberforce University. He then taught at the University of Pennsylvania, where he wrote the ground-breaking sociological study *The Philadelphia Negro* (1899). At Atlanta University (1897–1944) he developed a course of study on the life of black Americans and became head of the sociology department. In 1905 Du Bois helped found the Niagara Movement, which in 1909 became part of the emergent National Association for the Advancement of Colored People. He edited the NAACP journal, *Crisis*, from 1910 to 1932, demanding immediate enforcement of civil rights for blacks. In 1900 Du Bois called the first Pan-African Conference, demanding self-government for African colonies. His lifelong position was that blacks should develop their own cultural values. In furthering that cause, he became the leading black historian of the first half of the twentieth century, the author of major works including *The Souls of Black Folk* (1903), *Black Reconstruction* (1935), *Color and Democracy* (1945), and *The World and Africa* (1947).

Du Bois maintained a strained but cordial relationship with Washington during their lifetimes. At Washington's death in 1915, he referred to him as "the greatest Negro leader since Frederick Douglass, and the most distinguished man, white or black, who has come out of the South since the Civil War." Even so, he added, "in stern justice, we must lay on the soul of this man a heavy responsibility for the consummation of Negro disfranchisement, the decline of the Negro college and the firmer establishment of color caste in this land."

Not to be daunted by Washington's greater popularity and political influence, Du Bois summarized his own contribution in the statement: "I think I may say without boasting that in the period from 1910 to 1930 I was a main factor in revolutionizing the attitude of the American Negro toward caste. My stinging hammer blows made Negroes aware of themselves, confident of their possibilities and determined self-assertion."

Du Bois' disenchantment with the treatment of blacks in the United States led him to join the Communist party in 1961, after

Right: A street-car terminal in the segregated South during the Depression era.

which he emigrated to Ghana. He died at the age of ninety-five, in 1963, and was buried in Accra. The late Roy Wilkins, who served as executive secretary for the National Association for the Advancement of Colored People, states in his foreword to a new edition of *The Souls of Black Folk* that William Edward Burghardt Du Bois was prophetic in his statement that "The problem of the twentieth century is the color line."

The NAACP said of Du Bois' legacy: "He transformed the Negro world as well as a large portion of the liberal white world, so that the whole problem of relation of black and white races has ever since had a completely new orientation. He created what never existed before, a Negro intelligentsia, and many who have never read a word of his writings are his spiritual disciples and descendants. Without him the [NAACP] could never have been what it was and is."

THE NEED FOR BLACK SOLIDARITY

The precursor of the NAACP was the National American League, founded by Thomas Fortune, the black editor of the *New York Age*. Fortune organized 147 delegates from twenty-one states in Washington, D.C., in 1890 to discuss the black situation. Branches were soon organized in forty cities, with J.C. Price, the president of Lincoln University, serving as national president, but the movement was short-lived. It was succeeded in 1898 by the National Afro-American Convention, which started on a militant platform but shifted focus under the influence of Booker T. Washington.

Race riots occurred throughout the country in the early 1900s, including major incidents in Atlanta, precipitated by sensational news stories of a wave of rapes and murders allegedly committed by blacks. In Brownsville, Texas, black soldiers were insulted and drawn into confrontation. In New York City, violence broke out over competition between blacks and Irish immigrants for jobs and housing. Riots also occurred in Ohio, Indiana, and Illinois. The widespread rioting prompted African-American leaders to seek a united approach to combat discrimination, leading first to the Niagara Movement of 1905. Twenty-nine participants from four-

Left: *In Chicago, children set fire to a black residence during the Northern migration of the early twentieth century.*

The NAACP Nine-Point Program

Within a year of the 1910 establishment of the NAACP, a nine-point agenda of immediate priorities was adopted by its leaders:

1. To conduct a comprehensive study of the resources and performance of black schools.
2. To form a national Legal Redress Committee to combat racial discrimination within the judicial system.
3. To form a Bureau of Information to issue statements to the media and answer queries from individuals on black affairs.
4. To publish *The Crisis*, a monthly magazine, and pamphlets on the work of the committee.
5. To organize mass meetings and addresses on black affairs across the nation.
6. To form local action groups and "vigilance committees."
7. To lobby for the fair reapportioning of congressional districts.
8. To form a national committee to study aid to education.
9. To create international publicity, and participate in the Race Congress in London.

Right: Ida B. Wells, a famous speaker both at home and abroad, was best known for her antilynching work during the 1890s. She was editor and co-owner of the Memphis newspaper Free Speech.

teen states gathered in Fort Erie, Canada (to avoid discrimination), and agreed upon eight basic principles that were developed and extended during several meetings over a five-year period.

In 1910, the NAACP was formed. Its office, located in the *Saturday Evening Post* building on Vesey Street in New York City, was set up by Oswald Villard. The founding officers were Moorfield Storey, president; William E. Walling, chairman of the executive committee; John E. Milholland, treasurer; Oswald Villard, treasurer; Frances Bloscoer, executive secretary; and Dr. W.E.B. Du Bois (the only black officer), director of publicity and research.

The organization's original purpose was "to uplift the black men and women of this country by securing for them the complete enjoyment of their rights as citizens, justice in the courts, and equal opportunity in every economic, social, and political endeavor in the United States." Its first agenda items were enforcement of the Fourteenth and Fifteenth Amendments to the Constitution; right to education; right to vote; right to access in public places; and freedom from mob violence.

EARLY NAACP CAMPAIGNS

To combat the rising tide of lynchings (executions without due process of law), the NAACP established an antilynching committee and charged it with the responsibility of investigating individual murders, gathering data, and organizing political leaders and other spokespersons to address this issue. Thomas Fortune and Ida B. Wells were two leading black journalists whose writings aided the cause.

A white correspondent for the *Memphis News Scimitar* wrote the following description of a lynching he observed in Tennessee, in which a man was burned alive:

I watched an angry mob chain him to an iron stake. I watched them pile wood around his helpless body. I watched them pour gasoline on this wood. And I watched three men set this wood on fire. I stood in a crowd of 600 people as the flames gradually crept nearer to the helpless Negro. I watched the blaze climb higher and higher, encircling him without mercy. I heard his cry of agony as the flames reached him and set his clothing on fire. Soon he became quiet. There was no doubt that he was dead. The flames jumped and leaped above his head. An odor of burning flesh reached my nostrils. I felt suddenly sickened. Through the leaping blaze I could see the Negro sagging and supported by the chains.

To put an end to such barbaric acts, the NAACP launched a fund-raising campaign that generated more than ten million dollars. Despite widespread publicity and petitions to Congress, Southern politicians continued to block legislation against lynching. They also denied that these injustices were occurring. But what more could be expected from a region where the governor of North Carolina had announced at the end of Reconstruction: "We have solved the Negro problem. We have taken him out of politics and have thereby secured good government."

The NAACP was vigilant in overseeing violations of the Fifteenth Amendment. Moorfield Storey, the organization's first

Above: During the period 1910–35, the NAACP concentrated on bringing home the pervasiveness and barbarism of lynching to a largely ignorant population. These demonstrators picket a crime conference in Washington, D.C., in December 1934.

Above: The charismatic Marcus Garvey routinely wore his nationalist "uniform" of purple and gold for public appearances. In addition to his political campaigns, he led a religious movement, the African Orthodox Church.

The *Crisis* declared that residential segregation was unlawful, and in 1917 a Louisville, Kentucky, city ordinance upholding segregation in housing was declared unconstitutional. As a result of NAACP efforts, the Southern Railway Corporation agreed to employ blacks in skilled jobs in 1912. The NAACP also staged protests against D.W. Griffith's 1915 film *Birth of a Nation* in which he glorified the activities of the Ku Klux Klan.

National racial tension in the sports arena was displayed when Jack Johnson, a black boxer, became heavyweight champion in 1912. Anger and envy led to a riot that resulted in the death of eight blacks. The search for "the great white hope" occurred during the effort to dethrone the black champion.

Augmenting the NAACP's efforts to combat racism were those of the National Urban League, established in 1911 by black and white reformers. Booker T. Washington was instrumental in securing financial backing from wealthy whites, and the New York City–based League soon had branches in many major cities. The Urban League's initial purpose was to "improve the health, housing, job opportunities and recreation of city Negroes."

EMERGENCE OF NEW VOICES

The tone of passion was unmistakable in the voice of a black leader who rose to prominence after World War I: Marcus Garvey. A native of Jamaica who emigrated to the United States in 1917, Garvey was convinced that salvation for black people was tied to their return to Africa—a reprise of earlier colonization movements. In a speech entitled "An Appeal to the Soul of White America," Garvey explained his position:

The Negro must have a country, a nation of his own. If you do not intend to give him equal opportunities in yours, then it is plain to see that you mean that he must die, even as the Indian, to make

president, represented the NAACP in *Guinn v U.S.*, the case in which the Supreme Court ruled that the "grandfather clauses" in the state constitutions of Oklahoma and Maryland violated the Fifteenth Amendment (1915). Following the passage of the Nineteenth Amendment, which gave women the right to vote, the NAACP intensified its efforts to ensure greater participation by blacks in the electoral process.

room for your generations. Why should the Negro die? Has he not served America and the world? Has he not borne the burden of civilization in this Western world for three hundred years? Has he not contributed his best. . .? Surely all this stands to his credit, but there will not be enough room and the one answer is "find a place." We have found a place. It is Africa. And as black men for three centuries have helped white men build America, surely generous and grateful white men will help black men build Africa.

Garvey brought from Jamaica and reorganized his Universal Negro Improvement Association (UNIA), which developed black institutions and businesses, including the Black Star Line, a shipping company established to transport black Americans and West Indians to Africa. While many were critical of him and his grandiose costumes and entourage, his love for black people and his belief in their potential did much to raise black pride and awareness. His supporters poured some ten million dollars into the Garvey movement in a few short years, although black intellectuals called him a visionary and a demagogue. Garvey's dream of a mass exodus of blacks to Africa ended with his arrest and conviction for mail fraud in 1923.

Some of Garvey's critics, including A. Philip Randolph, had populist leanings of their own. The son of former slaves, labor leader Randolph organized the Brotherhood of Sleeping Car Porters and Maids in 1925. His frustration over racism led him to join the Socialist Party and to become coeditor of the radical *Messenger,* a magazine that took aim at domestic, economic, and social injustices. It was Randolph's vision that served as the impetus for the 1963 March on Washington.

The most notable recorder of this black history in the making was Dr. Carter G. Woodson, who published the first issue of the *Journal of Negro History* in 1916. He orga-

nized the Association for the Study of Negro Life and History and was the originator of Black History Month (originally Black History Week). Educated at Berea College, Kentucky, and the University of Chicago, Woodson received his doctorate from Harvard University in 1912 with the thesis "The Disruption of Virginia." His numerous books include *A Century of Negro Migration.*

Equally prominent in his own contribution was attorney Charles Hamilton Houston, who became the chief legal counsel for the NAACP in 1935. Born in 1895 in Washington, D.C., Houston was the only child of an upper-class family. After graduating from Amherst College, he taught English at Howard University, where he introduced a course in Negro Literature. Houston studied law at Harvard and later joined his father's law firm, where he took an altruistic approach and did much *pro bono* work for poor clients. Invited to return to Howard, he accepted and took on the challenge of reforming the law school. Here he trained some of the country's best legal minds, including the late Supreme Court justice Thurgood Marshall, a dominant figure in the landmark 1954 decision *Brown v Board of Education.*

Above: A. Philip Randolph, an influential activist from the 1920s until his death in 1979, planned a mass march on Washington, D.C., in 1941 to protest unfair employment practices.

BLACKS IN THE MILITARY

Although blacks realized that they would encounter the same racism in the military that they knew in civilian life, they were among the first to volunteer when the United States entered World War I in 1917. They served with honor, despite mocking reminders from the enemy that they were fighting for a freedom they did not know at home. Assigned laborious and dangerous tasks, they also suffered fascist directives, including one that forbade them to socialize with the French. Meanwhile, the black 371st Infantry Regiment was earning the Croix de Guerre for gallantry under fire.

As stories of the hardships and inequities black troops were facing reached the home front, the NAACP and other advocates took up their cause, demanding justice and fighting for integration. On July 28, 1917, more than ten thousand blacks marched down New York City's Fifth Avenue in the Silent Protest Parade. Organized by the NAACP under the leadership of Dr. Du Bois, they carried banners asking, "Mr. President, Why Not make America Safe for Democracy?" and "Thou Shalt Not Kill." Their protest included acts of violence against them in their own country that year, including brutal race riots in East St. Louis, Illinois, and Waco, Texas.

The following year, the NAACP published a pamphlet entitled "Thirty Years of Lynching in the United States," in which they documented that 3,224 persons had been lynched—2,522 of them black and 702 white.

THE 1920S AND '30S

The end of World War I brought an improvement in the economy, with middle-class blacks prospering, and a surge of creativity among black artists and intellectuals concentrated in Harlem, New York City, then the largest urban black community in the world. For the first time black culture was celebrated at a national level, including literature, music, and the theater arts.

On the political front, African-American Oscar DePriest of Chicago was elected to Congress in 1928, becoming the first black Congressman from a Northern state and the first black representative in the twentieth century. He would serve for three terms. Like Dr. Du Bois, DePriest articulated the suffering of black people everywhere. In a Congressional debate about American occupation and treatment of Haiti, he stated: "I am very glad to see the gentlemen on the minority side of the House so solicitous about the condition of the black people of Haiti. I wish to God they were equally solicitous about the black people of America."

The Communist Party attempted to attract disaffected blacks, but except for a few intellectuals, it was not successful. A common refrain among black people in the late 1920s was that it was "trouble enough being black without being Red as well." In 1929, with the onset of the Great Depression, this refrain would change to "last hired, first fired." Black unemployment in some cities soared to 70 percent. African Americans made a major shift from the Republican to the Democratic

Right: A prominent figure in FDR's New Deal, Mary McLeod Bethune. Her achievements included the founding of Florida's Bethune-Cookman College and directing Negro affairs in the National Youth Administration.

Party to help elect Franklin D. Roosevelt in 1932. Roosevelt and his wife, Eleanor, were strong supporters of civil rights, and many distinguished black Americans served in all four of Roosevelt's administrations, including Mary McLeod Bethune, William Hastie of Howard University, and Eugene Kinckle Jones of the Urban League.

Religion continued to be a major influence in the political and economic lives of African Americans. In Detroit, Elijah Poole took the surname Muhammad and helped found the Nation of Islam, popularly known as the Black Muslims, in 1931. This movement resembled Garveyism in its proclamation of pride, self-sufficiency, and self-help for African Americans, and was to become a significant force in the 1960s when Malcolm X helped popularize its message. Another important religious movement was that of the famous Father Divine, who drew many to his fold throughout the Depression with low-cost and free meals to all in need. Based in Harlem, he set up shoeshine parlors, grocery stores, restaurants, coal yards, and other joint efforts to benefit the poor, black or white. Father Divine advocated racial and economic equality under the slogan "Peace! It's truly wonderful!"

The National Labor Relations Act of 1935 encouraged the labor movement and, with it, a minimal degree of unity among black and white workers. Originally excluded from unions, African Americans only gradually recognized the benefits of unionization. In 1934 black and white farmers had organized to establish the Southern Tenant Farmers, with the goal of securing federal funds to prevent eviction from their land. A black sharecropper urged poor whites to cooperate with the words: "We don't have nothing against one another but we got plenty against the landlord."

Black sociologists contributed new insights with such publications as *The Free Negro Family* by Dr. E. Franklin Frazier, a professor at Howard University. Charles Johnson, editor of *Opportunity*, the voice of the Urban League, provided many young black writers and artists with the chance to publish for the first time. Walter White, who became secretary of the NAACP in 1931, also produced definitive and scholarly studies on the state of black America. In science, the arts, medicine, and politics, as Alain Locke put it, the black person "as a collaborator and participant in American civilization," had finally reached his "spiritual coming of age."

Left: African Americans fared worst in the search for employment during the Great Depression. Here, New York City police supervise the crowd lined up to register for Emergency Unemployment Relief.

PART II
"Were You There?"

New Challenges to Racism

"Education must not simply teach work—it must teach life."
—W.E.B. Du Bois, 1903

For African Americans, many gains were made during Franklin D. Roosevelt's years in office. He established numerous agencies to combat the Depression, including the Works Projects Administration (WPA), the National Youth Administration, the Civilian Conservation Corps, and the Federal Theatre. The WPA would affect the lives of more than 1,000,000 unemployed blacks. It enhanced black culture, added significantly to the facilities of black colleges and universities through the Public Works Administration, provided skilled trades to thousands, and opened up hundreds of non-traditional employment opportunities.

Artists employed through WPA projects included Claude McKay, Frank Yerby, Margaret Walker, Robert Hayden, Ralph

Ellison, and John H. Johnson (who later became publisher of *Ebony* and *Jet* magazines). Expatriate painter Henry Ossawa Tanner, whose primary works were religious in theme, was the dominant black painter until his death in 1937. His work was highly regarded among black artists, although intellectuals like Alain Locke admonished them to study African art for their cultural heritage. The WPA afforded many opportunities to do so. Author Richard Wright won the Federal Writers' Project prize in 1938 and two years later published *Native Son*.

WORLD WAR II

The NAACP and the Urban League joined forces in 1940 to protest black exclusion from defense industries. A. Philip Randolph lent support by proposing a March on Washington to demand defense-industry jobs and integration of the military, where black recruits were still segregated in the Army, limited to mess service in the Navy, and barred from the Air Corps and the Marines. The following year, Randolph and Walter White, secretary of the NAACP, met with President Roosevelt and top military officials to discuss their agenda. The promotion of Colonel Benjamin O. Davis, Sr., to the rank of brigadier general (the highest rank ever for a black officer in the U.S. Army) did not change the fact that the army was still segregated. It would remain so until 1948. However, to prevent the planned March on Washington and its possible consequences,

Opposite: Jackie Robinson, the first African American to play in baseball's major leagues, was an inspiration and a role model for black children.

Previous Pages: The historic 1963 March on Washington, as seen from the Lincoln Memorial.

Left: Colonel Benjamin O. Davis, Sr., brigadier general of the Negro Fighter Group, stands beside an F-47 Thunderbolt in 1940. His rank was the highest attained by a black officer in the U.S. armed forces to that date.

Above: A martyred champion of the civil rights movement, Medgar Evers was the first field secretary of the NAACP in the state of Mississippi.

"Twice a Patriot! Ex-Private Obie Bartlett Lost Left Arm—Pearl Harbor—Released: Dec., 1941—Now at Work Welding in a West Coast Shipyard." Heavyweight boxing champion Joe Louis was inducted into the army as a sergeant and appeared widely in publicity photos for the armed services. In 1940 the War Department agreed to set up a flight school for black pilots at Tuskegee. Eighty-two of the men trained there would be awarded the Distinguished Flying Cross. Black men also won their fight to be accepted into the Marine Corps, and black women joined both the WACs (Women's Army Corps) and the WAVES (Women Accepted for Volunteer Emergency Service), a branch of the U.S. Navy.

In total, more than 1,000,000 African Americans were inducted into the armed forces between 1941 and 1945; some half a million of them served overseas, in all branches of the services, including the Coast Guard and the Merchant Marine. Unfortunately, as during World War I, strife erupted on the home front in the form of race riots, including the devastating 1943 riot in Detroit that left thirty-four persons dead. Tensions around housing and relations in the workplace touched off the powder keg.

In their refusal to accept discrimination as usual, blacks returning from World War II helped pave the way for the civil rights movement. Too few jobs, inadequate housing, and social inequalities made them step forward and join the struggle for change. Membership in the NAACP increased rapidly, as these disenchanted veterans added their names to the rolls. And some of the white soldiers returning from the war sympathized with blacks and felt a moral obligation to break down racial barriers. One of them, Harry Ashmore, returned to the South and took a job as editor of the *Charlotte News.* He became a leading advocate for civil rights in North Carolina.

Roosevelt issued Executive Order No. 8802, which established the Fair Employment Practices Committee and banned discrimination in industries receiving government contracts. The wartime economy allowed many blacks to prosper, or at least to get on their feet. Exodus from the South resumed and reached pre-Depression levels, with some families choosing the West Coast, although the North remained the major destination.

One of the first heroes of World War II was black Navy cook Dorie Miller of the U.S.S. *Arizona,* one of the ships attacked at Pearl Harbor, Hawaii, on December 7, 1941. He seized a machine gun and shot down four Japanese planes, receiving the Navy Cross as a result. Black private Obie Bartlett was the subject of a wartime poster that proclaimed:

AFTER THE WAR: THE NAACP INITIATIVE

An early victory for the NAACP had been the Sweet case of the 1920s, which arose from mob action against Dr. Ossian H. Sweet, who had purchased a home in an all-white Detroit neighborhood. When Dr. Sweet's family attempted to move in, they faced an armed and hostile mob. Dr. Sweet fired into the crowd and a man was killed. Sweet, his wife, his two brothers, and seven other persons were arrested and charged with murder in the first degree. The NAACP had the help of Clarence Darrow for the defense and Dr. Sweet was acquitted. But the problem of discrimination in housing did not go away in Northern cities: It increased with black migration. Between 1940 and 1950, some 1.6 million blacks left the rural South. By 1950 Chicago had almost half a million black residents, Detroit, more than 300,000. Their families were still confined to ghetto like neighborhoods, not necessarily in substandard housing, but with restricted choices about where to live. Conversely, the increase in Northern black populations impacted favorably on black voting power, creating congressional districts that sent new representatives to the nation's capital.

By this time, the NAACP had become the premier civil rights organization in the country, as a result of painstaking labor in the fields of voter registration, education, employment, anti lynch laws, and a host of other arenas. The organization had been laying the groundwork for an assault on segregation in American schools since the 1930s, when Charles Hamilton Houston, vice-dean of Howard University's law school, began to travel through the South with his movie camera to record the appalling inadequacy of black schools vis-á-vis white. In 1935 Houston accepted the NAACP's invitation to direct the crusade against school segregation. Two years before, Nathan Ross Margold, a white

Harvard-trained NAACP lawyer, had developed the Margold Report, a legal strategy to challenge the constitutionality of *Plessy v Ferguson*. With the Margold Report as a guide, Houston started with professional and graduate schools. While nearly all Jim Crow states had separate white and black elementary and high schools by 1935, white planners had given little thought to the higher education of Southern blacks, expecting that few would seek such degrees. Black students of the segregated era grew accustomed to having their teachers leave during the summer months to attend graduate school in Northern cities. What few were aware of was that local state governments were paying these teachers to travel out of state rather than open the doors of all-white universities to them.

Above: Charles H. Houston, former dean of the Howard University Law School and chief counsel for the NAACP, in November 1939, when he was proposed to President F.D. Roosevelt as a candidate for the Supreme Court.

World War II At Home

Racial violence erupted on the home front during the summer of 1943. Northern cities were the venues. The influx of Southern blacks to work in defense industries touched off clashes around both employment and housing. Bombings, arson, and forced evictions followed.

In June terror stalked the streets of Detroit, where some 50,000 blacks had emigrated since 1941. As seen in these photographs, white hoodlums attacked unarmed blacks, overturned a black man's car—after dragging him out and beating him—then set the car on fire. The police took the side of white rioters, accosting blacks to search them for weapons and using guns and clubs indiscriminately. Twenty-five people were killed and more than three hundred injured.

In Harlem that August, black merchants protected their property with makeshift signs reading "Colored Store," as black youths—the majority in Harlem—vented their frustrations at Jim Crow in riots throughout the neighborhood. Hundreds were arrested and several died. At this time, almost 1,000,000 black men and women were serving in the armed forces.

The legality of this policy was tested when black candidate Donald Gaines Murray was denied admission to Maryland's all-white law school in 1935. Charles Houston was convinced that the 14th Amendment meant that states could not legally fulfill their requirement to provide equal access to black students by offering them funds to study out of their home states. Murray's case was brought to the attention of Houston by his former student Thurgood Marshall, then an attorney in Baltimore. Houston and Marshall argued the case and won Murray's admission to the University of Maryland, giving the NAACP its first victory against school segregation.

The following year they challenged the University of Missouri's refusal to admit Lloyd Lionel Gaines, a twenty-year-old black man, to law school. The State of Missouri told Gaines that they would build a separate school for him. Houston argued that it was inadequate to simply build a facility, call it a law school, and declare that this was equality. The court agreed and ruled that states had an obligation to provide equal education for their citizens. They could not send black students out of state instead of providing in-state facilities, nor could they ask students to wait for those schools to be built within the state. The significance of the Gaines ruling was its implication that states had the same legal obligations to black graduate students as to those in secondary and elementary schools. And beyond the matter of equality in education, there was the question of equal access to other public facilities.

Houston returned to his father's law practice in 1940, and Thurgood Marshall took on his role with the NAACP.

THE CONGRESS OF RACIAL EQUALITY

During and after the war, the Congress of Racial Equality (CORE), with black and white participants, staged nonviolent demonstrations against segregation in public facilities. The group was founded in 1942 by James Farmer, a member of the international peace group the Fellowship of Reconciliation. Members of CORE were often beaten and verbally abused, but they maintained their commitment to nonviolence. Bayard Rustin, who had been part of the labor movement with A. Philip Randolph, was CORE's first field secretary. As early as 1947, the organization traveled South on a "freedom ride" to test enforcement of the Supreme Court ruling (1946) that segregated seating of interstate passengers was unconstitutional. That "Journey of Reconciliation," as it was called, led to the arrest of some riders in North Carolina and their sentencing to a chain gang. During the 1960s, CORE would play a vital part in the Freedom Rides.

RADICAL STEPS FORWARD

Challenges to segregation in education continued with presentation of the crucial McLaurin and Sweatt cases by members of the NAACP Legal Defense Fund in 1950. Mailman Herman Sweatt had been refused admission to the University of Texas Law School at Austin in 1946. Professor G.W. McLaurin, then sixty-eight years old, had been refused admission to a doctoral program in education at the University of Oklahoma. When a special district court ruled that he must be admitted, he was required to sit at a desk surrounded by a railing marked "reserved for colored." Both cases

reached the Supreme Court on appeal and were ruled upon on June 5, 1950.

Abandoning the demand for equal schools under the "separate-but-equal" doctrine, the NAACP challenged the constitutionality of segregation itself. In its 1950 rulings on McLaurin and Sweatt, the Court did not overturn *Plessy,* but did emphasize that "separate-but-equal" education was not just a slogan:

Above: Despite warnings to keep away from the polls, African Americans turned out in full force to cast their ballots in the Georgia Democratic primaries on July 17, 1946.

Left: Professor George Washington McLaurin, a graduate student in education, admitted to the University of Oklahoma at Norman by court order, is relegated to an anteroom apart from white students. The NAACP took his case to the Supreme Court via the Legal Defense Fund in 1950.

Separate But Equal?

The one-room schoolhouse of frontier days was still in use at mid-twentieth century—for rural Georgia's black children. This scene was replicated across the South from Reconstruction until after the 1954 Supreme Court ruling that separate educational facilities for black and white citizens were unconstitutional.

Two landmarks of black higher education, both founded in the nineteenth century, were Howard University, Washington, D.C. (right) and Tuskegee Institute in Tuskegee, Alabama (opposite). Howard University, now a multiracial institution, received a government charter during Reconstruction, when only one black person in ten among the newly freed could read or write. It has produced scholars and teachers of renown, including historian Rayford W. Logan and sociologist E. Franklin Frazier. It was at Howard's law school that NAACP attorneys practiced for their arguments before the Supreme Court in *Brown v. Board of Education*. The Tuskegee Institute, founded by Booker T. Washington, was built by its rural black students, who came to learn farming, animal husbandry, and various trades that would help them establish their own businesses and benefit their communities.

Right: Professor Kenneth Clark of City College of New York, and his wife Mamie Phipps, both psychologists, devised a series of tests using black and white dolls to demonstrate how children perceived themselves. The results confirmed that segregation contributed to low self-esteem among black children and resultant psychological damage. During the 1960s, Dr. Clark became known as an outspoken critic of the white liberal establishment.

equality involved more than physical facilities, and black students could not be segregated, harassed, or otherwise restricted when they were admitted to state universities.

Marshall and his colleagues at the Legal Defense Fund resolved to extend their attack on segregation as unconstitutional. To prove that separate schools could never be equal, the NAACP needed to show the psychological, intellectual, and financial harm that resulted from them. They began by developing comparative studies of per capita spending on education of black as opposed to white students, of physical facilities, and of student to staff ratios. The results were similar to South African studies on education under apartheid.

A test case against segregation in elementary schools as harmful to black children was presented in federal district court in late 1950. Although three times as many black students as white attended elementary school in South Carolina's Clarendon County, whites received more than 60 percent of the educational funds. Per capita spending for white students was $179 per year, for blacks, $43. Twenty black parents from the county, led by a local pastor, the Reverend J.A. DeLaine, brought suit through the NAACP. Harry Briggs, the father of five, was the first on the list: thus

the case was called *Briggs v Clarendon County*. The Briggs family, like so many brave blacks across the South, would pay for their place in history with daily harassment, loss of employment, and danger to their lives.

Expert witnesses retained by Marshall, Robert Carter, and their colleagues were the psychologists Kenneth Clark and his wife, Mamie Phipps. They had used black and white dolls in test studies in Washington D.C. (1939), New York City (1940s), and all over the South to evaluate how children perceived themselves. The NAACP asked them to conduct such tests in Clarendon County. Black children were asked to choose the doll they liked best, the one who looked most like them; the "nice" one and the "bad" one (information the children volunteered), and other related questions to gauge their sense of self-worth.

The results indicated overwhelmingly that segregation contributed to the development of low self-esteem and consequent psychological damage, but the federal district court ruled that the separate-but-equal rule had not been violated in Clarendon County. The lone dissenting voice was that of white judge J. Waties Waring, who wrote: "Segregation in education can never produce equality and...is an evil that must be eradicated."

BROWN v BOARD OF EDUCATION OF TOPEKA

Encouraged by Judge Waring's support, Legal Defense Fund lawyers pressed on to the next case, in Topeka, Kansas. There, the Reverend Oliver Brown complained that his seven-year-old daughter, Linda, had to cross the railroad tracks to attend an inferior school across town while there was a good school—all-white—much closer to home. Thus black church leaders have fearlessly stepped forward throughout the struggle for civil rights. Undoubtedly, this was a leap of spiritual faith for many, but the

The Radical Ministry

Black clergymen were in the forefront of the civil rights movement from the beginning. They were arrested in Montgomery, Alabama, on June 22, 1956, for violating the law banning boycotts. Among the sixty-eight demonstrators taken into custody that day (pictured below) were, from left, the Reverend Ralph D. Abernathy of the First Baptist Church; his colleague Reverend Garer; Rufus Lewis, manager of the Citizens Council; the Reverend Leroy R. Bennett, president of the Interdenominational Council; the Reverend W.F. Alford of the Beulah Baptist Church; the Reverend J.H. Cherry of the Jericho A.M.E. Church; and the Reverend H.H. Herbert of the Bethel Baptist Church.

In Nashville, Tennessee, a year later, the Reverend Everett W. Jackson was arrested for "pulling a gun on white demonstrators" when he escorted parishioners Linda Gail McKinley and her mother, Mrs. Grace McKinley, to newly integrated classes at a local school. A day later, Nashville's nearby Hattie Cotton School was gutted by a dynamite explosion.

practical element was involved as well, since black ministers were among the few whose economic survival was not tied to the local white establishment. Even so, it took tremendous courage for all the Browns and Briggses in small Southern towns to put their names and families on the line.

Two leading attorneys who assisted Marshall in this case were Robert L. Carter and Jack Greenberg. As they developed *Brown,* other NAACP attorneys were litigating cases bearing on school segregation across the country. One of them began when a black student, Barbara Rose Johns, led a strike by fellow students at Moton High School in Prince Edward County, Virginia, in April 1951. Johns had witnessed endless efforts by black parents to get improvements for their local school. Taking matters into her own hands, she mobilized fellow students to strike as a protest against conditions at Moton High. She won the support of NAACP attorney Spottswood Robinson, who challenged parents of the striking students to stand with their courageous children. A month after the two-week strike, Robinson filed *Davis v County School Board of Prince Edward County* asking that Virginia abolish its mandate of segregated schools. (The first of the 117 names on the petition was that of Dorothy E. Davis, the fourteen-year-old daughter of a Prince Edward County farmer.)

The Klan burned crosses in the yard of the Johnses' home. To guard her safety, young Barbara was sent to Montgomery, Alabama, to live with her uncle, Vernon Johns, the minister of Dexter Avenue Baptist Church. A civil rights activist, Johns laid the foundation for the work of his successor at Dexter, the Reverend Martin Luther King, Jr. Johns was one of the first to challenge Jim Crow transportation laws in Montgomery.

Two other school cases in litigation as the court continued to delay hearings on *Brown* were *Bolling v Sharpe,* a District of Columbia case in which the NAACP challenged separate-but-equal directly, and a Delaware case, *Gebhart v Belton.* The Supreme Court announced that it would hear *Briggs v Clarendon County,* with *Brown v Board of Education of Topeka,* in the fall of 1952. On October 3, the court

added *Davis v Prince Edward County*, and two weeks later, *Bolling v Sharpe* and *Gebhart v Belton*.

On December 11, six days after the hearings opened, deliberations began. Nine months passed, during which presiding chief justice Fred M. Vinson died of a heart attack. Earl Warren was nominated by President Eisenhower as his replacement. On Monday, May 17, 1954, Justice Warren delivered the historic ruling, which read in part:

> *We cannot turn the clock back to 1868, when the [Fourteenth Amendment] was adopted, or even to 1896, when Plessy versus Ferguson was written. We must consider public education in the light of its full development and its present place in American life throughout the nation. Only in this way can it be determined if segregation in public schools deprives these plaintiffs of the equal protection of the laws.*
>
> *Does segregation of children in public school solely on the basis of race, even though the physical facilities and other 'tangible' factors may be equal, deprive children of the minority group of equal educational opportunities? We believe it does.*
>
> *In the field of public education the doctrine of 'separate but equal' has no place. Separate educational facilities are inherently unequal.*

The decision was unanimous. A year later, the court ordered that public schools be desegregated "with all deliberate speed."

In the main, African Americans celebrated: much labor and sacrifice had gone into achieving this victory in the most important civil rights case of the century. Still, there was legitimate concern in some quarters as to what would become of the many black educators and traditional black institutions. Anthropologist Zora Neale Hurston was one of the brave voices that publicly challenged the notion that black children needed to sit beside white children in a classroom to be well educated—a position for which she would receive harsh criticism.

BACKLASH

Predictable anger and opposition was the reaction of white Southern segregationists. A kind of white-collar Klan, the Citizens' Council, made up of businessmen, bankers, and other so-called respectable whites, was formed in Indianola, Mississippi, the most

Below: Members of the National States Rights Party petition Alabama's state government to close the schools rather than integrate (1963).

segregated and supremacist bastion of the Deep South. Branches spread across the region. A leading spokesperson for the Citizens' Council was Yale-educated Tom Bradley, a Mississippi circuit judge, who wrote: "When a law transgresses the moral and ethical sanctions and standard [of the majority], invariable strife, bloodshed and revolution follow in the wake of its attempted enforcement. The loveliest and purest of God's creatures, the nearest thing to an angelic being that treads this terrestrial ball, is a well-bred, cultured Southern white woman or her blue-eyed, golden-haired little girl. We say to the Supreme Court and to the northern world, 'You shall not make us drink from this cup...We have, through our forefathers, died before for our sacred principles. We can, if necessary die again.'" This overwrought appeal to white fears of miscegenation was joined to pressure in many familiar forms. The Citizens' Councils used denial of credit and/or employment for anyone complying or associating with persons who complied with the decision. Mob violence resulted in beatings, burnings, and lynchings.

Some districts in the North and Upper South desegregated without incident. Black and white students began attending school together for the first time in cities like Baltimore and Washington, D.C. But in the Deep South, diehards in state government vowed resistance. One was Governor Herman Talmadge of Georgia, who had previously banned books on blacks from the classroom and dismissed two white professors from the University of Georgia for their involvement with the Julius Rosenwald Fund (which supported education for blacks across the South). Talmadge immediately denounced *Brown* and declared it worthless. In defiance of the Supreme Court, he announced that Georgia "would not tolerate the mixing of the races in the public school or any other tax-supported institution." Talmadge's sentiment was shared by fellow Southern lawmakers in Congress, ninety-six of whom drew up the "Southern Manifesto," in which they, too, denounced the decision and set plans in motion to repeal it. Other Southern resistance groups that emerged included: The American States' Rights Association; Federation of Constitutional Government; Federation of Defenders of State Sovereignty and Individual Liberties; The Grass Roots League; National Citizens' Protective Association; The States' Rights Council of Georgia, Inc.; The Society for the Preservation of State Government and Racial Integrity; and the Virginia League.

In 1955 the Supreme Court, over the objections of the NAACP, adopted the "go slow" approach to integration as proposed by the Justice Department. Although *Brown* had called for immediate integration, the Justice Department decided erroneously that a gradual pace might circumvent Southern politicians' attempts to defy authority and curtail the rise of resistance groups. In fact, while several hundred schools had integrated in 1954, only thirty-nine were added in 1955. Lerone Bennett describes this period as a battle zone:

> And so the war began. There were three lynchings in Mississippi in 1955. Two NAACP leaders [both clergymen] were slain because they refused to take their names off voter registration lists. In the fall of 1956, skirmishes were fought at Sturgis and Clay, Kentucky, where National Guard units were called out to escort black children through the lines of howling mobs. The Tennessee National Guard was sent to Clinton to put down an uprising by white demonstrators....A dynamite blast destroyed Nashville's Hattie Cotton Elementary School, which had 388 white and one black student.

Black men, women, children—there were no gender or age barriers to the deep-seated racial hatred unleashed as my generation came of age in the South. Black parents protected

children as best they could, reluctant to create too much fear in them and thereby rob them of the peace and wonder of childhood. Children attempting to drink from a "white only" fountain or relieve themselves in a segregated restroom were hurried in a different direction without comment. Black teenage girls were told "never" to sit up front when driven home from evening baby-sitting jobs for white families. And under no circumstances were girls to go with unknown white males, who sometimes cruised black neighborhoods with fictitious offers of housework or child care. Stories abounded of young girls from poor neighborhoods being raped after they were deceived into believing they would earn money for chores. These stories were repeated by parents and teachers, lest some other black girl be victimized.

When black families had the choice of sending only one or two children of their large families to college, daughters were often chosen over sons—the parents reasoning that boys could escape the segregated South through military service, if by no other means. But their daughters, they were convinced,

Left: Southern theaters maintained separate entrances and ticket booths for black patrons.

Opposite, above: The nation's capital was one of the first cities to comply with the order to desegregate. At Thompson Elementary School, some of the city's 98,000 children attend classes together for the first time on September 13, 1954.

Opposite, below: The federal elementary school at Fort Myer, Virginia, for children of military personnel, conducted biracial classes for the first time on September 7, 1954, by order of the U.S. Department of Defense. Virginia's public schools remained segregated.

Signs of the Times

Jim Crow cast a long shadow across the South that no black citizen could safely ignore. From Reconstruction through the 1950s, "colored" drinking fountains, restrooms, beaches, rooming houses, and other facilities were clearly labeled and their counterparts were off-limits by law. The degrading message, repeated over generations, impaired black self-esteem and dulled the sensibilities of the majority to pervasive injustice.

The price of admission at the back entrance to Pensacola, Florida's Saenger Theater — or any theater of its kind — was identical to the one paid at the front.

The 1956 photograph of Airman 2nd Class Philip Wagner of New York City at Atlanta's railroad terminal, en route to Warner Robbins Air Force Base near Macon, shows passive compliance with the recent Interstate Commerce Commission ruling against segregated interstate travel facilities. Beneath the sign that reads "Colored Waiting Room," the words "Intrastate Passengers" (within Georgia) have been added.

needed all the assistance a family could provide to help them rise above the circumstances of their second-class existence.

Black parents stayed prepared. They took their own socks "uptown" when going to the shoe store so they wouldn't have to use the dirty sock passed to Colored people who came to try on shoes. They packed boxes of fried chicken and other food when traveling, for they knew there would be no stopping at a restaurant on the road. And unbeknownst to most outsiders, nearly every black family owned a gun. Children learned the Southern mores of yielding sidewalk space and other social practices of their elders' daily lives. It was not so unbearable to say "ma'am" and "sir" to white adults, as this was a courtesy black children extended to all adults, regardless of race. However, it was unpleasant to hear white children disrespect black adults, whom their parents referred to as "girl" or "boy."

Innocence, and sometimes the pretense of not knowing any better, allowed black children to forego these so-called courtesies. My own father commonly referred to the handicapped white man whom he served as a "helper" simply as "C.L." around our home. But C.L., or "Mister C.L." (as, it turned out, he assumed we called him) rode up to our house one day in his specially equipped car and asked me to get my father. "Daddy, C.L. out here!" I called, and dashed off to continue playing.

I had no idea that I had done anything wrong, but later I heard my father tell my mother that his boss had been disturbed by my familiarity. "Them chil'ren of yours," my father said, laughing as he mocked his employer, "they ain't got no bizness callin' me by my firs' name." Daddy told Mama that he had responded by saying, "Now Mr. C.L., I figure I hafta say Mr. to you, but what my children do and say ain't got nothing to do wit' us."

I don't recall my mother's response, but I'm sure she gave my father stern warning against filling our heads with such boldness. For the experience of my mother as it related to white authority was, tragically, one of great fear. Vigilante attacks by whites on blacks that she had witnessed played havoc with her psyche. She shared stories of the terror that occurred in small Georgia towns, where even as late as the 1950s, black adults lived under curfew rules. Fiercely guarding the safety of her children, my mother encouraged us to follow Jim Crow laws to the letter. The fear that resided in her was in the hearts of the black women of her generation who had grown up in the South.

THE EMMETT TILL CASE

Mamie Bradley, the mother of Emmett Till, lived in Chicago, but she had been born in Mississippi's Delta region. So she understood clearly the possibility of danger to a young black boy who made what Southern whites would perceive as a wrong gesture, or spoke an "incorrect" word. With this in mind, she gave her fourteen-year-old son

Left: Fourteen-year-old Emmett Till of Chicago, whose murder by white racists in Money, Mississippi, in the summer of 1955 shocked the nation into a new awareness of the consequences of racial hatred.

Emmett forewarning of the "ways of the South" before she sent him to visit relatives at the home of Moses Wright, near Money, Mississippi, for the summer. It was the relative freedom of having grown up in the North, and the typical playfulness of a teenage boy, that made Emmett show off in front of his cousin and friends.

He had brought with him photos from his junior high school graduation in Chicago, which showed both black and white students. Seeing that the Southern children were impressed, Emmett commented that one of the white girls in the photos was his girl friend. This prompted one of the local boys to say, "Hey, there's a white girl in that store there. I bet you won't go in there and talk to her." Calling the boy's bluff, Emmett went in, bought some candy, and as he was leaving the store, said to the woman, "Bye, baby."

Hunted down by the woman's husband, Roy Bryant, and his half-brother, J.W. Milam, the following Saturday night, Emmett Till was kidnapped from his relatives' house, savagely beaten, shot, and thrown

Above: Emmett Till's great-uncle, Moses ("Mose") Wright, holds some of Emmett's clothing after his body was found to demonstrate that he was "a large boy for his age."

Right: Emmett's mother, Mamie Bradley, collapses in the Chicago railroad terminal at the sight of her son's casket. Ministers of her church support her.

into the Tallahatchie River with a seventy-five-pound cotton gin fan attached to his neck by barbed wire. Blacks who testified at the trial of the two white men, which began on September 19, 1955, were hurriedly rushed out of town by the NAACP for their safety. In a trial that lasted five days, the all-white jury (who heard attorneys for Bryant and Milam state in summation, "I'm sure that every white Anglo-Saxon one of you has the courage to free these men!") deliberated for only one hour before setting the defendants free, despite the courageous testimony of Mose Wright, who pointed out the two murderers at the risk of his life.

The horror of the Till incident drew national attention. So did the shock of the other bodies dredged up from the river in the search for Emmett Till. The murders of ministers George Lee and Lamar Smith had been committed at about the same time in the Delta region. Lee, the first black to register to vote in the town of Belzoni, was killed by a shotgun blast in the face: Town authorities ruled it a traffic accident. Lamar Smith was shot in broad daylight in front of the Brookhaven Courthouse one week before Till's death. No arrest was made in either case, nor was there widespread news coverage.

Had Emmett Till's mother not insisted on having his body returned to Chicago, and dared to expose the mutilated corpse before the world, his death might have gone unnoticed. The thirty-three-year-old woman collapsed on the platform of the train station when the child's casket arrived, crying, "Lord, take my soul." On the first day that the casket was open for viewing, thousands lined the streets outside the Rainier Funeral Home. Thousands more attended the funeral on September 3. And millions saw the terrible photograph published by *Jet* magazine.

Civil rights leader Medgar Evers, who served as field secretary for the NAACP in Mississippi, was responsible for getting witnesses and evidence for the Till murder case and for securing safe passage from Mississippi for the witnesses. Sadly, he would be murdered himself in Mississippi in 1963, by white supremacist Byron de la Beckwith. Two trials ended in hung juries and the charges against Beckwith were dropped, despite compelling evidence of his guilt. A third trial ended in his conviction.

Below: Widowed Myrlie Evers and her three children mourn the assassinated Medgar Evers, Mississippi field secretary for the NAACP. Shot in the doorway of his home in 1963, he had been on a nine-man death list circulated by white extremists.

No Justice

Sumner, Mississippi, September 1995: In a trial that lasted only five days, the killers of Emmett Till were set free, despite overwhelming evidence of their guilt. At left, the boy's great-uncle, Moses ("Mose") Wright, points to defendants Roy Bryant and J.W. Milam and announces, "There they are." Deputy Sheriff John E. Cochran (below, left) examines the cotton-gin fan that was attached to Emmett's neck by barbed wire before his body was thrown into the Tallahatchie River. Below, Mrs. Mamie Bradley, Emmett's mother, is subpoenaed to testify at the trial. Seated in the foreground (opposite, top) are the members of the all-white jury selected to decide the fate of the accused. Roy Bryant with his family at the trial (opposite, below left), where he defended himself by stating that the murdered boy had "wolf whistled" at his wife. (Opposite, below right) Bryant and his half-brother, J.W. Milam, greet the news of the Verdict "Not Guilty."

Montgomery to Mississippi

"We must do something and we must do it now."

—Ida B. Wells, 1928

On December 1, 1955, Rosa Parks, a forty-two-year-old black seamstress, refused to comply with the demand of a Montgomery, Alabama, bus driver that she give up her seat to a white man and move to the back of the bus—the Colored Section. This defiant act would soon lead to the successful year-long Montgomery bus boycott, which earned Mrs. Parks the title "Mother of the Civil Rights Movement."

Rosa Parks was not the first African American to be arrested for defying Montgomery's segregated-bus policy, but she was the ideal rallying point for the black community's offensive against discriminatory practices in public transportation and the Jim Crow system as a whole. Mrs. Parks, a Methodist, was secretary of Montgomery's NAACP chapter and one of its Youth Council Advisers.

THE HIGHLANDER FOLK SCHOOL

As though to prepare for her day of decision, Mrs. Parks had studied civil disobedience at the Highlander Folk School in Monteagle, Tennessee, a training ground for civil rights activists. Founded in 1927 by Myles Horton, Highlander was an integrated institution where progressive people gathered for

Opposite: Rosa Parks, heroine of the civil rights movement for her role in the successful Montgomery bus boycott of 1955–6.

Below: Dr. King was labeled a communist sympathizer for taking part in biracial workshops on nonviolent social action.

The "Communist Threat"

Segregationists took advantage of postwar paranoia about communism for their cause. The anticommunist hearings conducted by Senator Joseph R. McCarthy in 1954 served as an imprimatur. In August 1957, the woman and child shown at right demonstrated in front of the Arkansas capitol building in Little Rock, appealing to Governor Orval Faubus and Christian Fundamentalist interpretations of the Scriptures to fight the proposed integration of city high schools.

A photograph of Martin Luther King, Jr., taking part in biracial workshops on nonviolent protest at the Highlander Folk School in Monteagle, Tennessee, was used to identify the institution on a billboard (previous page) as a "Communist training school." Communism and liberal Christianity were linked again when Nashville schools began to integrate in September 1957. Picketers and police greeted black women enrolling their children, and white parents began a boycott of the school (below). The picketers bore signs with quotations from both the Old and New Testaments taken out of context ("Intermarriage Is Accursed") or reworded to support their fears of miscegenation and integration.

workshops on social reform. It functioned as a center for the "Social Gospel," and was one of the few places in the South where blacks and whites mixed freely.

Theologian Reinhold Niebuhr, who had taught Myles Horton at Union Theological Seminary, served as chairman of Highland's advisory board, which at various times included Norman Thomas, a Socialist and Presbyterian minister; Harry Emerson Fosdick, an ordained Baptist minister who taught at Union Theological Seminary and served as pastor of New York City's Riverside Church; and Eleanor Roosevelt, humanitarian, writer, and lecturer.

Myles Horton came up with the idea for Highlander while working as a summer student in an impoverished Tennessee community. He had grown up in Appalachia and believed that people did not need to be told about their problems and how to solve them;

instead, they needed the opportunity to articulate their own ideas and work out solutions. In short: People are not powerless.

Mentored by Reinhold Niebuhr, Myles Horton studied utopian communities and was influenced by philosopher John Dewey, whose works include *Liberalism and Social Action* (1935). His initial focus was on labor issues, including the right to unionize. Highlander's statement of principle (1932) read in part: "The purpose of the Highlander Folk School is to assist in creating leadership for democracy. Our services are available to labor, farm, community, religious and civic organizations working toward a democratic goal."

Mrs. Parks was encouraged to attend Highlander by someone who had been impressed by her NAACP work: Virginia Durr, the wife of attorney Clifford Durr, who hired Mrs. Parks as a seamstress for the couple's daughters. Clifford Durr, who was related by marriage to Supreme Court justice

Left and below: Two prominent activists who participated in conferences at Highlander. James Bevel (left), a powerful spokesman for the Southern Christian Leadership Conference, emphasizes a point at a mass meeting on behalf of voter registration. A talented musician, Bevel also popularized many of the songs that became identified with the movement. Stokely Carmichael (below), chairman of the Student Non-Violent Coordinating Committee, on the Mississippi Freedom March in June 1966. Carmichael was there fresh from a successful voter registration drive in Lowndes County, Alabama (between Selma and Montgomery).

Right: The Reverend Mohandas Gandhi, called "Mahatmú" (Great-Souled) by the Indian people for his spiritual and political leadership. He developed the tactics of nonviolent civil disobedience that forced Great Britain to grant independence to India in 1947 and that were emulated by black leaders of the civil rights movement.

Hugo Black, had many political acquaintances (including Lyndon and Claudia "Lady Bird" Johnson) from his Washington days as FCC Commissioner. These relationships were strained during the 1950s, when he resigned his post to defend victims of the Joseph R. McCarthy hearings, whom the FBI labeled as communists and traitors. Durr and a fellow Montgomerian, Aubrey Williams (who had served as executive director of the National Youth Administration from 1935 to 1943), were among the original sponsors of Highlander.

Besides Rosa Parks, numerous other black leaders passed through the school, including the Reverend Martin Luther King, Jr., and his colleagues, ministers Ralph Abernathy, Andrew Young, and James Lawson; Mrs. Septima Clark, who led citizenship classes on John's Island; and Ms. Ella Baker, organizer and executive director for the Student Nonviolent Coordinating Committee (SNCC), founded in 1960. SNCC activists Julian Bond, Stokely Carmichael, John Lewis, and James Bevel all participated in Highlander conferences. It was a Nashville quartet led by James Bevel that introduced many songs that became thematic of the movement at Highlander. And folk singer Guy Carawan added to the repertoire

with songs that evolved from the 1930s labor movement: "We shall Not Be Moved," "Keep Your Eyes on the Prize," "This Little Light of Mine," "I'm Gonna Sit at the Welcome Table," and "We Shall Overcome." The spirit of Highlander energized many black and white college students to participate in the sit-ins that began in the fall of 1959 and spread across the country.

LOCAL LEADERSHIP

Mrs. Parks's role in the Montgomery boycott began as she returned from her job at the Montgomery Fair Department Store, where she would be dismissed for her involvement in the boycott. She deliberately took her seat in the front of the bus; when threatened with arrest by the driver, she replied politely, "You may do that." Upon her arrest, she called her mother, who in turn called Montgomery's leading black political activist, Edward Daniel "E.D." Nixon, a retired Pullman porter and head of the Progressive Democrats (who opposed the all-white Democrats of Alabama). Nixon also led the local chapter of both the NAACP and the Brotherhood of Sleeping Car Porters and Maids, and he was probably influenced in his tactics by the union's radical founder, A. Philip Randolph. Nixon called the police station to inquire about Mrs. Parks and was told by the desk sergeant that it was "none of [his] damn business." He turned to Clifford and Virginia Durr, who were known for their support of black rights. After making bond for Mrs. Parks, Nixon and the Durrs returned home with her. Seeing the opportunity to use this incident as the test case for challenging segregation in city transportation, Nixon and Durr conferred with Rosa Parks.

In Montgomery more than 75 percent of bus patrons were black: most whites were car owners. Yet black people were subjected to the daily humiliation of entering the bus to pay their fares, then leaving to re-enter the back of the bus. If the white section filled up, they had to yield their seats to white people. Previous attempts to violate the status quo in Montgomery had failed to generate enough black support to be successful. Not this time.

Jo Ann Robinson, a college English teacher and leader of the black Women's Political Council, stayed up until four o'clock in the morning mimeographing 50,000 protests, delivered on December 2 to schools, businesses, and other locations with the help of student volunteers. Nixon called black spokesmen, including the new pastor of the Dexter Avenue Baptist Church, the Reverend Martin Luther King, Jr., and enlisted their support for a possible boycott of the buses. King agreed to consider it and promised to help when Nixon called back later. "I'm glad," said Nixon, "because I already set the meeting up to meet at your church." Other black ministers, including the Reverend Ralph Abernathy, of the Brick-A-Day Baptist Church, joined the cause.

THE REVEREND MARTIN LUTHER KING, JR.

Born January 15, 1929, in Atlanta, Georgia, to a Baptist minister's family, Martin Luther King, Jr., was educated at Morehouse College, Crozier Theological Seminary, and Boston University. Seeking a way to relate spiritual values to social needs, he studied the writings of India's Mohandas Gandhi, whose nonviolent resistance to British rule helped impel India to achieve independence. Gandhi's willingness to suffer rather than inflict harm was entirely consonant with King's Christian heritage and his admiration for philosophers Henry David Thoreau and Walter Rauschenbusch. In 1849 Thoreau's essay "Civil Disobedience" had stated unequivocally: "Under a government which imprisons any unjustly, the true place for a just man is also a prison." It was his commitment to non-

violence that would make King the preeminent leader of an irresistible moral force.

The Montgomery bus boycott began on December 5 and triumphed a year later because black citizens simply refused to ride the city buses. Under the auspices of the Montgomery Improvement Association (MIA), they organized car pools, walked to work, hitchhiked, and bicycled. They started an ad hoc taxicab company and resisted high pressure from city officials in the form of parking and traffic tickets for imaginary infractions. White citizens accused blacks of organizing "goon squads" to keep fellow blacks off the buses: it was hard for them to believe that Jim Crow could be defied in such numbers. Robert Weisbrot, the author of *Freedom Bound*, states that motorcycle policemen were assigned "to trail every bus and keep on the lookout for harassment of potential riders. That first day a college student helping an elderly woman across the street was seized for 'intimidating passengers.' But the fact was that no one—from the 'goon squads' of the city's imagination to officials trying to break the boycott—was intimidating Montgomery's aroused black citizens."

Right: The Reverend Martin Luther King, Jr., takes his seat at the front of the bus after the successful boycott in Montgomery (December 23, 1956).

Above: The Reverend Martin Luther King, Jr., urges calm after a bomb damaged his home in Montgomery during the bus boycott. No one was injured in the blast.

Right: Two weeks after the bus boycott ended, the home of the Reverend Ralph Abernathy (right) was also heavily damaged by a bomb.

This page: Signs of Victory: A Dallas Transit Company worker removes the notice demanding segregated seating on city buses after the Supreme Court ruling against discrimination on public transportation (April 1956, left). Montgomery buses roll again without the stigma of separate passenger sections (below, left). Black and white passengers ride together in Norfolk, Virginia, for the first time (below).

Right: Virgil Hawkins was forty-eight years old before he won his fight for admission to the University of Florida law school in March 1956. At that time, he was public relations director for Bethune-Cookman College in Daytona Beach.

The city finally attempted to break the boycott through the county courts, but while deliberations were going on, news came of the December 1956 Supreme Court decision that voided Montgomery's law to segregate buses. Late in December, the first black riders took their seats with little opposition. News of the victory empowered African Americans across the country, and boycott leaders became focal points for a host of civil rights activists in search of direction.

"DELIBERATE SPEED"

When school reopened in September 1956, almost 2.5 million black children were still in segregated schools. Only about 800 Southern school districts, with some 320,000 black children, had complied with the *Brown* ruling. Deep South states including Virginia, North

Below: Autherine Lucy becomes the first black student to enroll at the University of Alabama— February 1, 1956.

and South Carolina, Georgia, Florida, Mississippi, Louisiana, and Alabama were united in their determination to fight integration.

Autherine Lucy, a sharecropper's daughter, had attempted for three years to enroll at the University of Alabama, Tuscaloosa, as a student in library science. She was finally admitted by order of the federal district court and attended her first class as the university's first black student on February 3, 1956. Three days later, riots broke out on the campus as the dean of women drove Lucy between classes. A thousand men pelted the car, made threats against her life, and stoned the house of the president. Lucy was suspended from the university. The Birmingham federal court ordered her reinstatement on February 29, but university trustees met and expelled her on a trumped-up technicality. It would be almost ten years before another black applicant was accepted. Elsewhere, resistance took various forms, ranging from token integration to blatant defiance on the part of Southern officials. Both black and white schools were bombed in Atlanta. Newsmen of both races were attacked by mobs when they tried to cover school openings. On June 15, 1959, the *New York Times* reported that "resistance groups, typified by the White Citizen's

Council born in Mississippi in 1954, have spread across the South.... Gunpowder and dynamite, parades and cross burnings, anonymous calls, beatings and threats have been the marks of their trade."

LITTLE ROCK

In September 1957, nine black teenagers sought to register at Central High School in Little Rock, Arkansas. Their admittance was opposed by the state's governor, Orval Faubus, who sent members of the Arkansas National Guard to bar their way. The move to integrate Little Rock schools was spearheaded by NAACP state president Mrs. Daisy Bates, copublisher with her husband of the black weekly *Arkansas State Press*. Ms. Bates planned to accompany the nine young people to school on the first day, September

Above: Mrs. Daisy Bates, president of the Arkansas NAACP, with her attorney, Robert L. Carter, pursues her appeal against charges brought by the Little Rock Municipal Court in connection with her activities on behalf of school integration.

Left: A large crowd gathers at Little Rock's Central High School, as National Guardsmen prepare to prevent black students from entering to register on September 3, 1957.

The Little Rock Nine

These Arkansas teenagers made history in the fall of 1957, when they persisted in their efforts to enroll in Little Rock's all-white Central High School. Pictured below, from left (seated on floor) are Thelma Mothershed, Elizabeth Eckford, and Melba Pattillo; seated above, Jefferson Thomas, Ernest Green, Minniejean Brown, Carlotta Walls, Terrence Roberts and Gloria Ray. More than 1,000 members of the 101st Airborne Division were sent to Little Rock to protect these students during September. In October, the federalized Arkansas National Guard assumed the task.

Minniejean Brown (left) is photographed smiling as she enters school under armed guard. Remarkably, all nine students consistently maintained their composure despite the hostile environment and daily harassment, until, after three months, Minnijean at last responded to a taunt. She tipped her lunch on the aggressor and was promptly expelled from the school.

Arkansas NAACP leader Daisy Bates played a heroic part in the integration struggle. In August 1958, Ms. Bates is shown escorting seven of the now famous Little Rock Nine on a tour of the White House (opposite).

4, but she failed to reach the parents of Elizabeth Eckford because they did not have a phone, so Elizabeth set out on her own.

Eckford recalled in *Eyes on the Prize* how she walked toward the entrance of the school, hoping that the presence of the National Guard would dissuade the crowd of raging white racists from attacking her.

"The crowd began to follow me, calling me names," she recalled. "I still wasn't afraid—just a little bit nervous. Then my knees started to shake all of a sudden and I wondered whether I could make it to the center entrance a block away. It was the longest block I ever walked in my whole life. Even so, I wasn't too scared, because all the time I kept thinking the [guards] would protect me."

As Eckford attempted to enter, the guards, who were giving passage to white students, blocked her. "I walked up to the guard who had let [the white students] in. He, too, didn't move. When I tried to squeeze past him, he raised his bayonet, and then the other guards moved in and raised their bayonets. Somebody started yelling, 'Lynch her! Lynch her!'"

Desperately seeking a friendly face, Elizabeth looked toward an elderly white woman, whom she first saw as a sympathizer, only to have the woman spit on her. "No nigger bitch is going to get in our school!" she heard from the crowd. "Get her out of here!"

Spotting a bench at the bus stop, Elizabeth ran toward it with the mob in pursuit, and sat down as new threats to lynch her rose from the crowd. It was a Northern reporter, Benjamin Fine of the *New York Times*, who offered comforting words. Lifting her chin, he told her gently, "Don't let them see you cry." Grace Lorch, a white woman whose husband taught at a local black college, stepped forward to rescue Elizabeth from the mob and accompanied her home. After Day One, no black student attempted to enter Central High alone.

In explaining her desire to attend Central High School, Melba Pattillo Beals told *Eyes on the Prize* interviewers that the school had better equipment and greater opportunities for those who aspired to attend college. "I did not have an overwhelming desire to integrate this school and change history," she stated. Of her daily concerns at the time, she explained: "I worried about silly things, like keeping my saddle shoes straight, what am I going to wear today—things that a fifteen-year-old girl does worry about, but also, which part of the hall to walk in that's the safest. Who's going to hit me with what? Is it going to be hot soup today? Is it going to be so greasy that it ruins the dress my grandmother made for me? How's this day going to go?"

The black students were subjected to name-calling, thrown objects, shoving, tripping, harassing phone calls to their homes, and death threats. One among them, Minniejean Brown, was finally worn down. First she was suspended for pouring a bowl of chili over the head of a boy who was harassing her with taunts of "nigger, nigger, nigger!" She was then expelled in February 1958 for calling another taunter "white trash." Minniejean moved to New York City, where she completed high school.

Ernest Green, who had transferred to Central as a senior, recalled, "It seemed an opportunity to participate in something new. In the spring of '57, before we left school for the summer, each teacher gathered names of interested students. I put my name in, and that's where I left it...I talked with my mother about it. She said if I wanted to go and I was accepted, she would support me. People like my mother and grandfather, who was a postman and had attempted to vote in the Democratic primary, really are the backbone of the southern resistance. They didn't take a high public position, but in many ways expressed their indignation, their anger, and

attempted to turn things around. My mother and my aunt were part of a lawsuit in the 1940s that filed for equal pay for black and white teachers. We kids did it mainly because we didn't know any better. But our parents were willing to put their careers, their homes on the line. To me that says a lot."

Like most of the black students who were pioneers of integration, Ernest Green had to

Left: Troopers of the 101st Airborne Division patrol the grounds at Central High School late in September 1957.

Opposite, above: Pursued by a jeering mob, fifteen-year-old Elizabeth Eckford attempts to register at Central High, only to be turned back by Arkansas National Guardsmen.

Opposite, below: The U.S. Army convoys the Little Rock Nine to school.

Below: Ernest Green becomes the first black student to graduate from Little Rock's Central High School on May 27, 1958.

face the heartbreak of the social limitations that came with departure from his all-black school. "You knew that you weren't going to play football, be in the band or the class play, go to the prom," he points out. "I had been in the school band for five years, from seventh grade through eleventh. Tenor sax. But this was an important enough breakthrough that all of these other activities, well, you could give them up." Ernest Green survived these losses to become the first black graduate of Central High School, on May 27, 1958.

It had taken a Supreme Court edict and a presidential proclamation, along with the 101st Airborne Division of the U.S. Army and a contingent of the state militia, federalized to ensure the children's safety, to accomplish integration at Central High. Over the next three years, the Bateses' home was bombed repeatedly and riddled with bullets. Their newspaper was forced to close, and forty-four teachers who sided with the forces of integration were fired.

By 1962 all the city's high schools had been forcibly desegregated: its elementary schools remained separated by race. Perpetrators of mob violence, readily identifiable from film footage and photographs, were neither arrested nor prosecuted by the U.S. Attorney involved or the Department of Justice. The message that mobsters could "get away with murder" was heard all over the South—at lunch counters, houses of worship, public transportation, and voting booths.

JAMES MEREDITH AT "OLE MISS"

In 1962 twenty-nine-year-old U.S. Air Force veteran James H. Meredith underwent the acid test of integration: enrolling at the state university in Oxford, Mississippi. He first consulted with NAACP leader Medgar Evers about transferring from all-black Jackson State in 1961, and Evers enlisted the aid of the Legal Defense Fund. On September 3, 1962, a federal district court ordered the University of Mississippi to

Right: Face-off: Meredith (left) after his enrollment at the University of Mississippi on October 1, 1962, over the strident objections of Mississippi governor Ross Barnett (right).

Early in 1957, the Southern Christian Leadership Conference (SCLC) had been formed by Martin Luther King, Jr., Bayard Rustin, and Stanley Levinson to coordinate the activities of nonviolent groups working for black civil rights. The movement was constantly in the news after the Montgomery boycott, and in 1960 the forces of protest would be strengthened by the participation of black and white students who had been coming of age since the *Brown* decision. As one of them, Bernard Lee, said when he was expelled from his college by order of the governor of Alabama for civil rights activism, "Education without freedom is useless."

Left: NAACP attorney Constance Baker Motley was instrumental in securing Meredith's enrollment at "Ole Miss."

Below: Meredith scans the headline of the New Orleans States-Item story on his attempt to enter the University of Mississippi— September 25, 1962.

admit James Meredith, and the Kennedys were committed to enforcing the ruling.

Flanked by NAACP attorneys Constance Baker Motley and Jack Greenberg, Meredith was blocked by state governor Ross Barnett, who physically barred his way into the school, asserting that he would die before permitting a black student to attend "Ole Miss." Federal troops were dispatched to Oxford, and riots erupted on the campus. several federal marshals and soldiers were wounded, and two men were killed. To shouts of "Kill the nigger!" Meredith registered and attended classes—escorted by 15,000 soldiers.

In 1963 James Meredith became the university's first African-American graduate. Three years later, he was wounded by a shot in the back on U.S. Highway 51, as he made a "one-man pilgrimage against fear" from Memphis to Jackson. Dr. King and other protesters took up the march until Meredith was able to continue.

Whites Boycott Schools

In February 1959 twenty-one black teenagers, including, below, from left, Frank Grier, James Kilby, and Fay Coleman, were the only students attending the Warren County High School (capacity 1,000) in Front Royal, Virginia. Reopened on February 18 by federal court order, the school was boycotted by white parents who were determined to maintain segeregated schooling.

In New Orleans, six-year-old Ruby Bridges (left) became the first black child to enter the William Frantz Elementary School since Reconstruction (September 1960). She was almost alone there with her teachers throughout the school year. New Orleans white parents who tried to break the boycott in support of school integration, like Mrs. James Gabrielle, were jeered at by other parents who had withdrawn their children (center). Meanwhile, children from New Orleans' newly integrated McDonogh Elementary School were transported by bus to nearby St. Barnard Parish to continue their segregated education (November 1960, opposite, left).

In Birmingham, Alabama, integration of Graymont School (opposite, right) did not take place until September 1963. An angry white parent protests by withdrawing her son from the school.

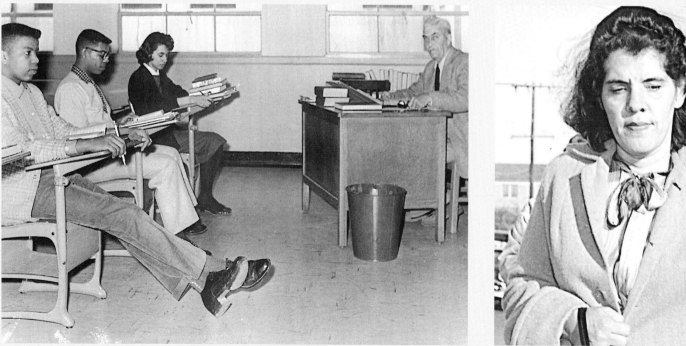

The Children's Miracle

Courageous—and terrified—black children from Brooklyn to Birmingham conducted themselves with impressive dignity in the face of jeers, screams, racial epithets, spitting, and physical attacks. Fifteen-year-old Dorothy Geraldine Counts (left) endures taunts as she walks to Harding High School in Charlotte, North Carolina, in September 1957. She was pelted with pebbles and trash as she left the building. In Queens, New York, September 1959, black students transferred from Brooklyn's Bedford-Stuyvesant section into Public School 68 (below), one of five Queens schools widely boycotted by white parents.

Mothers of white students scream (opposite, left) as three black children enter McDonogh Elementary School, New Orleans (1960). The school was boycotted by white parents in the wake of outbreaks of violence in the city. The evils of hatred and bigotry were ingrained at a young age: These children (opposite, right) could hardly have understood the symbolism of this 1956 demonstration. Die-hard segregationist students in Birmingham protest after integration of the city's West End High School (opposite, below, in 1963).

We Shall Not Be Moved

"That day, for a moment, it almost seemed that we stood on a height, and could see our inheritance; perhaps we could make the kingdom real, perhaps the beloved community would not forever remain that dream one dreamed in agony."

—JAMES BALDWIN, 1963

Four freshmen at North Carolina Agricultural and Technical College, a black school in Greensboro, spent a lot of time together in the fall of 1959 asking themselves and each other what they could do about the racial barriers that held them back and mocked federal edicts against discrimination. Five years after the *Brown* decision, 99 percent of Southern black children still attended segregated schools. In 1957 Congress had affirmed the voting rights of all citizens regardless of race, yet only 3 per-

cent of eligible blacks in Mississippi were registered voters. The signs of separation— Jim Crow signs—were everywhere: "For White Only," "Colored Entrance," "Colored Area," "Colored Beach," "Room for White," "Colored Taxicab Stand." Drinking fountains, rest rooms, even outhouses were labeled. The four young people on the Greensboro campus—Ezell Blair, Jr., David Richmond, Joseph McNeil, and Franklin McCain— moved gradually from discontent to resolution. There must be something *they* could do.

Opposite: Two protestors attempt to evade the high-pressure fire hoses used to disperse demonstrations in Birmingham, Alabama, in May 1963.

Below: Seated left and next left are Joseph McNeil and Franklin McCain, two of the original lunch-counter demonstrators.

THE "SIT-INS" BEGIN

Encouraging their resolve was a white storekeeper and NAACP member, Ralph Johns, who was known in Greensboro for his friendship with black customers and his support for their civil rights. Johns proposed that the four students defy the ban on interracial dining by sitting down at the "white" lunch counter at the local Woolworth's and placing an order. They did this on February 1, 1960. The store manager ignored them, and a white policeman paced behind them, visibly angry and upset, but making no move to arrest them. Other Woolworth's customers reacted with emotions ranging from vilification to encouragement. Several elderly white women patted them on the back, and one of them said, "Ah, you should have done it ten years ago." They were not served but they returned to school elated.

Below: Two students from St. Augustine College are ignored by waitresses as they stage a sit-in at this white-only restaurant in Raleigh, North Carolina. Following several such demonstrations, lunch counters at three downtown Raleigh stores were closed down in 1960.

The following day, twenty other A&T students joined the protest. Three days later, they were joined by the first white students. The "sit-ins" spread to half a dozen other North Carolina communities, and their range extended to shopping centers, drugstores, theaters, drive-ins, and other public facilities. When reporters asked the four initiators, "How long have you been planning this?" they answered spontaneously, "All our lives!"

The movement spread rapidly to campuses across the South, and Northern students crossed the Mason-Dixon line to lend their support. Train and bus stations were affected, as black students took their seats in "white-only" waiting-room sections. Local custom was disrupted by read-ins at segregated public libraries, kneel-ins at churches, and wade-ins at public swimming pools.

The students won widespread support from established and newly formed civil-rights organizations, including the NAACP, CORE, the Southern Christian Leadership Conference, led by Martin Luther King, Jr., and the Student Nonviolent Coordinating Committee. But nonviolence was often met by attack. the *New York Times* reported of one incident that "Whites armed with ax handles, baseball bats, and other weapons set upon black youth. Intermittent rioting followed. Other riots have taken place in Portsmouth, Va., and Chattanooga, Tenn." That year, almost half the NAACP's annual budget went toward defending some 1,700 student demonstrators standing trial. The charges ranged from trespassing to conspiracy in restraint of trade. Julian Bond, a bright, charismatic student at Atlanta University, went to jail with his friends repeatedly.

Above: Professor John R. Salter (seated left) was sprayed with ketchup and mustard by these teenagers who then beat him on the back and head, in Jackson, Mississippi, May 28, 1963.

Left: Some of the fifty lunch-counter demonstrators who were arrested under a 1958 anti loitering ordinance in Chattanooga, Tennessee, after they refused the manager's request to leave.

BOYCOTTS AND PICKETING

As in Montgomery in the middle '50s, boycotting was implemented to good effect. Blacks used their buying power to deal only with integrated restaurants and shops. Some stubbornly segregated businesses failed in the South, and Northern branches of chain stores with discriminatory Southern outposts were picketed. Combined boycotts and sit-ins impacted upon the integration of public facilities in many Deep South cities, including Atlanta, Nashville, and Dallas—but there was a price to pay in bloodshed, imprisonment, attacks by police dogs, and harassment by the Ku Klux Klan. Despite these provocations, most of the demonstrators adhered closely to the ethos expressed by Dr. King: "The objective was not to coerce but to correct; not to break wills or bodies but to move hearts." These efforts added much to the cause.

Right: One week later, a protestor demonstrates outside Woolworth's in Lynchburg, Virginia. NAACP spokesman Reverend Virgil Wood stated that picketing would continue until all downtown stores agreed to desegregate their lunch counters.

A Show of Support

Beginning in 1960, demonstrators in both North and South picketed merchants, including the powerful Woolworth chain, who practiced lunch-counter segregation in many of their stores. In Atlantic City, New Jersey, scene of the protest shown below, labor union members and private citizens joined in supporting the first sit-ins, in North Carolina, March 1960, and urging shoppers to boycott stores that endorsed discrimination. The power of the boycott was felt nationwide. North Carolina's NAACP spokesman, the Reverend Virgil Wood, insisted that picketing would continue until Woolworth's and other downtown stores agreed to serve blacks at their lunch counters. The boycott tactic, effective in Montgomery's 1957 bus desegregation campaign, was used extensively during the civil rights years. In April 1963 (left, in New York City), during the Birmingham campaign for voting rights, demonstrators protest Dr. Martin Luther King's imprisonment and reinforce organized labor's support for desegregation nationwide.

The Kennedy/Nixon Campaign, 1960

Neither Senator John F. Kennedy nor Vice-President Richard M. Nixon entered the 1960 presidential campaign with an impressive record on civil-rights issues. However, Nixon's eagerness to win the Southern Democratic vote exceeded his expectations from black voters, and he alienated most of them before the November election. His lone black staff member was kept at a distance and excluded from key decisions, and his press secretary vehemently denied a claim that Nixon was a member of the NAACP. Kennedy, on the other hand (pictured here during a campaign stop in New York City), pursued the black vote with energy, relying on the sound advice of such liberal aides as his brother-in-law Sargent Shriver, the prominent black Democrat Louis Martin, and Harris Wofford, a Southern white activist with strong civil-rights credentials. Kennedy's poise and presence during the televised debates with Nixon (below), although the subject of civil rights was scarcely touched upon, made a favorable impression on voters nationwide. Black voters saw real promise for their cause in his New Frontier agenda, and in his remarks upon accepting the nomination, in which he referred to the "peaceful revolution" that was "demanding an end to racial discrimination in all parts of our community life." The African-American vote was a decisive factor in Kennedy's narrow election victory.

KENNEDY FOR PRESIDENT

LEADERSHIP FOR THE 60's

THE FREEDOM RIDERS

In 1961 the Freedom Riders took up the cause of testing interstate transportation facilities, where segregation had been ruled illegal by the Interstate Commerce Commission—a ruling that was blatantly ignored all over the South. Bus stations not only had separate waiting areas and ticket windows for black passengers, they often had no restroom for them. In some cases, one restroom designated "Colored" had to be used by both men and women. Black passengers could not obtain service at rest-stop lunch counters. Again, it was black students in the South who led the way, soon joined by members of CORE, FOR, and other nonviolent civil-rights groups who rallied to their support.

Fisk University college student Diane Nash was twenty years old when she became a leader of the sit-ins at Nashville, Tennessee's, department store lunch counters and the Nashville Student Movement. She selected the Nashville contingent for the Freedom Rides to Birmingham; Montgomery; Jackson, Mississippi; and New Orleans—destinations where the protesters were met by mobs and police brutality. The newspapers were filled with photographs of bleeding Freedom Riders who had been set upon by outraged Southerners with the tacit approval of city officials. An incendiary bomb was thrust into one of the buses in Anniston, Alabama, and several people were injured. The bus was destroyed. White demonstrator James Zwerg,

Above: A Greyhound bus carrying the first Freedom Riders was firebombed outside Anniston, Alabama, on May 15, 1961. Several of the stunned passengers were injured in the blast.

Above: Freedom Riders John Lewis (left) and James Zwerg, victims of the mob attack at the Montgomery bus station.

Opposite: Two days after the attack on the Freedom Riders, national guardsmen patrol the sidewalk in front of the Montgomery bus terminal (above). Below, the bus leaving Montgomery for Jackson, Mississippi, escorted by sixteen highway patrol cars.

Right: Freedom Riders inside Montgomery bus station's white-only waiting room.

attacked by a mob at the Montgomery bus terminal, was refused passage to the hospital in a white ambulance. In Mississippi, Governor Ross Barnett backed the Jackson police department, which greeted Freedom Riders with immediate arrest—150 were brought to trial on a single day. People were illegally held at Parchman Penitentiary when the city jails overflowed, and exorbitant fines were imposed.

In the 1960 presidential election, black voters had comprised an important bloc in the close race between John F. Kennedy and Richard M. Nixon. Sixty-eight percent of the black vote went to the young Democratic candidate, who won by only two-thirds of one percent of the popular vote. But Kennedy introduced no new civil-rights legislation and failed to make good his promise to eliminate discrimination in federally funded housing projects. The Freedom Riders put pressure on the Kennedy administration to enforce the ICC ruling against segregated transportation facilities, which had been restated by the Supreme Court in December 1960. Support from the North came from CORE, whose executive director, James Farmer, explained his Freedom Ride strategy to Juan Williams, author of *Eyes on the Prize* : "What we had to do was to make it more dangerous politically for the federal government *not* to enforce federal law than it would be for them to enforce federal law....We decided the way to do it was to have an interracial

group ride through the South....We felt we could count on the racists of the South to create a crisis."

The crisis was forthcoming in May 1961, not long after the groups left their point of departure—the nation's capital—bound for Alabama and then Mississippi. Attacks on the riders occurred at Rock Hill, South Carolina, and Anniston, Alabama, where the incendiary bomb destroyed one of the two buses. At Birmingham, the riders were assaulted by thirty men armed with baseball bats, lead pipes, and bicycle chains. No policemen appeared. When reporters inquired why, Public Safety Commissioner T. E. "Bull" Connor replied that it was Mother's Day, so he was short on staff. Connor had allegedly promised the Ku Klux Klan fifteen minutes in which to savage the riders to the point where "it looked like a bulldog got a hold of them."

The president and his brother, Attorney General Robert Kennedy, were annoyed by the news that more Freedom Riders were prepared to embark after the first battered contingent was flown to New Orleans. But to avoid additional mob violence, a force of 500 federal marshals was dispatched to the next stop, Montgomery, narrowly averting a possible massacre at Ralph Abernathy's Baptist church, where Dr. King had appeared to support the demonstrators.

Robert Kennedy's intervention with Senator Eastland of Mississippi, primarily to avoid a political fiasco, averted mob violence in the state Freedom Riders had most dreaded to enter. However, over time, hundreds were arrested (with federal government consent) for traveling with "the avowed purpose of inflaming public opinion." Police brutality went undercover—in Jackson's prisons and in Parchman Penitentiary's maximum-security wing, where the robust James Farmer lost thirty pounds. Roy Wilkins of the NAACP called Farmer's strategy "desperately brave."

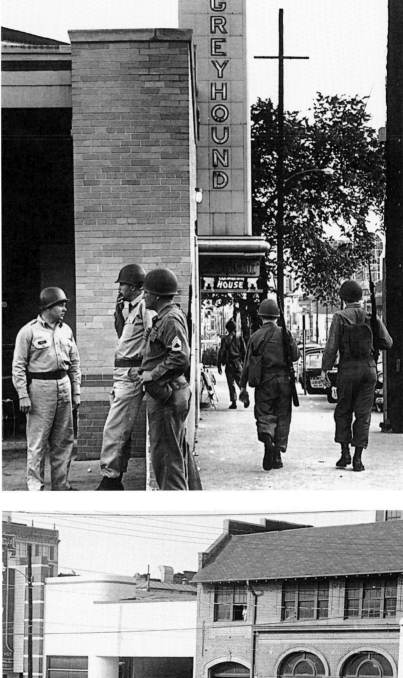

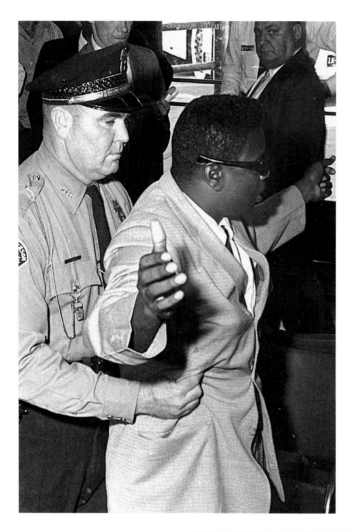

The SNCC Statement

Between 1960 and 1961, the student protest movement swept the nation, shaking the public from its long complacency. The statement formulated by the Student Nonviolent Coordinating Committee read in part: "We affirm the philosophical or religious ideals of nonviolence as the foundation of our purpose, the presupposition of our faith and the manner of our action. Nonviolence as it grows from Judaic-Christian traditions seeks a social order of justice permeated by love. Integration of human endeavor represents the crucial first step towards such a society.

Through nonviolence, courage displaces fear; love transforms hate. Acceptance dissipates prejudice; hope ends despair. Peace dominates war; faith reconciles doubt. Mutual regard cancels enmity. Justice for all overthrows injustice. The redemptive community supersedes systems of gross social immorality.

Love is the central motif of nonviolence. Love is the force by which God binds man to Himself and man to man. Such love goes to the extreme; it remains loving and forgiving even in the midst of hostility."

Above: Upon arrival in Jackson, the Freedom Riders were greeted by policemen who took them directly to jail.

Right: Among those arrested in Jackson was John Lewis, whose bandage covers a wound inflicted in Montgomery.

THE ALBANY MOVEMENT

Late in 1961, King's SCLC came to Albany, Georgia, to lead a protest campaign after five SNCC workers were arrested. A coalition of local groups had persisted in its efforts to desegregate terminals and open biracial talks with town officials. Unfortunately, King's arrival created tensions among the various protest groups, especially the students of SNCC, who wanted to take a bolder line. Roy Wilkins, leader of the NAACP, would recall: "We paid some of the expenses of the Albany movement, only to be insulted for being on the wrong side of the generation gap."

Albany police chief Laurie Pritchett, too cunning to bring out the fire hoses and police dogs in view of the national media, took the same approach as his Mississippi counterparts. Demonstrators were "peacefully" arrested, then subjected to beating, dirty cells, and other forms of abuse off-camera. Hundreds of arrests were made. In July 1962, Dr. King returned to Albany with Ralph Abernathy and voluntarily went to jail rather than pay the fine for his "illegal" protest in

December. Volunteers converged on Albany to demand King's release, and the mayor promptly freed him and his fellow prisoner, Dr. Abernathy. They were practically ejected from the city jail. As Abernathy remarked about the ulterior motive for their release, "I've been thrown out of lots of places in my day but never before have I been thrown out of jail." Subsequent events in Albany only deepened the rift between local civil-rights factions and national leadership of the movement.

THE BIRMINGHAM CAMPAIGN

Voter registration was the cause of new violence in September 1962, when President Kennedy denounced the burning of churches in Georgia to discourage black voter registration drives. Apart from his reluctant decision to use federal troops to enroll James Meredith at the University of Mississippi that same month, the president had shied away from decisive action on behalf of the movement. A new crisis was needed to force the government's hand. Thus the SCLC

Below: Outside City Hall in Albany, Georgia, more than sixty demonstrators kneel in prayer for a just verdict in the hearing of eleven jailed Freedom Riders, who were arrested in December 1961. After refusing Mayor Asa Kelley's order to disperse, several of these peaceful protestors were arrested.

"Bombingham"

Birmingham, Alabama's largest city, had the reputation among civil rights activists as the "worst big city in the U.S.A." Eighteen unsolved bombings in black neighborhoods between the late 1950s and 1963 gave it its nickname. On the front lines was Fred L. Shuttlesworth, the activist black minister of the Bethel Baptist Church.

When state officials banned the NAACP in Birmingham after the bus boycott, Shuttlesworth organized the Alabama Christian Movement for Human Rights (ACMHR). His home was destroyed by a bomb in 1956, and no arrests were made. The following year, the courageous minister and his wife attempted to register their two daughters, Ricky and Patricia, in an all-white school: They were greeted by mobs shouting obscenities, and the parents were viciously attacked.

By 1963 the devastation following a bomb attack was an all-too-familiar sight in Birmingham (below). A tearful woman kneels in prayer during the demonstrations of May 1963 (left). National publication of scenes like these helped build consensus for the "Second Reconstruction."

planned its campaign against segregation in Birmingham, which had stubbornly resisted every order to comply with demands for integration. Local SCLC affiliate Dr. Fred Shuttlesworth worked closely with Dr. King to plan sit-ins and marches, raise funds for bail in case of mass arrests, and teach nonviolent techniques in the city's black churches.

The protests began in downtown Birmingham on April 3, 1963, under the baleful eye of Police Commissioner "Bull" Connor, who held his fire for several weeks, during which Dr. King was imprisoned and held in solitary confinement for three days. During this period, he wrote the powerful "Letter from Birmingham Jail," drafted April 16 on scraps of paper with a pen smuggled in by a black trusty. The document was printed as a pamphlet by the American Friends Service Committee, a Quaker peace group, and widely excerpted in the media. It read in part:

But when you have seen vicious mobs lynch your mothers and fathers at will and drown your sisters and brothers at whim; when you have seen hate-filled policemen curse, kick, brutalize and even kill your black brothers and sisters with impunity; when you see the vast majority of your twenty million Negro brothers smothering in an air-tight cage of poverty in the midst of an affluent society; when you suddenly find your tongue twisted and your speech stammering as you seek to explain to your six-year-old daughter why she can't go to the public amusement park that has just been advertised on television, and see tears welling up in her little eyes when she is told that Funtown is closed to colored children, and see the depressing clouds of inferiority begin to form in her little mental sky, and bitterness toward white people; when you have to concoct an answer for a five-year-old son asking in agonizing pathos: "Daddy, why do white people treat colored people so mean?"; when you take a cross-country drive and find it necessary to sleep night after night in the uncomfortable corners of your automobile because no motel will accept you; when you are humiliated day in and day out by nagging signs reading "white" and "colored"; when your first name becomes "nigger" and your middle name becomes "boy" (however old you are) and your last name becomes "John," and when your wife and mother are never given the respected title "Mrs."; when you are harried by day and haunted by night by the fact that you are a Negro, living constantly at a tip-toe stance, never quite knowing what to expect next, and plagued with inner fears and outer resentments; when you are forever fighting a degenerating sense of "nobodiness"; then you will understand why we find it difficult to wait.

This impassioned plea for justice strengthened the resolve of the Birmingham protesters, and several days after King was released on bail, all hell broke loose in the city. Hundreds of adolescents and younger children had been recruited by May 2, and they took to the streets with enthusiasm. More than 900 of them were arrested that day. Next day the march to City Hall was aborted when police barricaded the Sixteenth Street Baptist Church, with a thousand protestors inside. Those who attempted to leave were assaulted with fire hoses set to a pressure that would strip off tree bark, clubbed indiscriminately, and attacked by police dogs. The carnage shocked the nation as scenes from the war in Vietnam would do soon afterward.

Young black men in the city's poorest sections repudiated nonviolence and rioted against their oppressors. White merchants faced a sea of black picketers and protestors who discouraged patronage of their stores. Fearing an all-out race war, Birmingham began to capitulate, over the disavowals of Governor George Wallace. On May 12, President Kennedy ordered 3,000 U.S. Army troops to the city limits and prepared to federalize the Alabama Guard.

Audrey Faye Hendricks, nine years old and in the third grade, was one of the children arrested on May 2. Later, she would recall: "I wasn't nervous or scared. We started at the Sixteenth Street Church. We always sang when we left the church. The singing was like a jubilance. It was release . . . it also gave you calmness and reassurance. We went down . . . by Kelly Ingram Park and marched about half a block. Then the police put us in paddy wagons. There were lots of kids, but I think I may have been the youngest child in there."

The policemen later segregated Audrey Faye to interrogate her about the march. They pressed for details of the plans and suggested that she had been forced to participate. "I was nervous when they first called me in,"

Right: Wielding a nightstick, a Birmingham police officer chases this defenseless demonstrator, whose clothes are soaked from an encounter with the fire hoses.

she remembers. "The worst thing I thought was that they might kill me. After they started asking me questions, I calmed down a little and thought, maybe they're not going to do anything. But it crossed my mind. It was a room of five or six men. All white. And I was little..."

After being questioned, Audrey was finally returned to her cell, where she remained jailed with other children for seven days. "We slept in little rooms with bunk beds...about twelve of us to a room. We called ourselves Freedom Fighters. The food wasn't home cooking. I remember some grits, and they weren't too good. My parents could not get word to me for seven days."

As demonstrations continued, news came that the cells were all full and that the police were now forced to take students to the fairgrounds to house them. "I felt like I was helping to gain freedom," Audrey continues. "At the end of seven days, they told me my par-

ents were there to get me. I was real glad. They were just smiling and hugging me. I knew they had been nervous 'cause I heard them on the phone talking to friends and saying, 'Oh, I'm glad she's back!' I could tell they were proud of me."

Another student, Myrna Carter, remembers a "well-dressed old white lady who walked up [to the young protestors] and said, 'Why don't you niggers go back to the North? The niggers here is satisfied.' She didn't know who we were. You know, they called it 'Northern interference.' They didn't have sense enough to know that we were not from the North. They thought we didn't have enough guts to do that, so it had to be someone from the North. She didn't touch me or spit on me. She just made that statement and walked off."

Myrna Carter's account ends with the march by youths and adults who lined up in pairs and headed for Memorial Park on May 6. Bull Connor awaited them with his fire-

Above: *Some of the youngsters arrested in Birmingham for parading without a permit wave proudly from the school bus transporting them to jail. On May 2, 1963, more than 900 demonstrators, most of whom were under eighteen, were arrested.*

men and their hoses and policemen with their dogs on leashes. The police would taunt the demonstrators by allowing the dogs to lunge forward, then pulling them back.

"When we got to Memorial Park, Reverend [Charles C.] Billups [a local minister] was standing in front of the group, and he said, 'We are ready for your fire hoses, your dogs, and anything else!' And tears just started running down his face. Bull Connor told the firemen, 'Turn the water on! Turn the water on!' But they stood there frozen. 'Turn the water on!' Then he started using profanity, cursing them, shaking the hose and shaking them. 'Turn the hose on! Turn it on!' But those people just stood there. They would not turn the hoses on that Sunday. Then the whole group [of protestors] started singing Negro spirituals. It was just something in the air."

Shortly thereafter, bombings, riots, and other forms of violence ceased. Local merchants took down their Jim Crow signs, and the city's new mayor, Albert Boutwell, repealed the municipal segregation laws. Blacks were hired for positions that had never been open to them before. The Birmingham campaign and the other protests it generated over the next seven months involved more than 100,000 people and created the political and emotional climate that empowered the movement's greatest demonstration.

THE MARCH ON WASHINGTON

On June 20, 1963, President Kennedy met with civil-rights leaders who were planning the largest political assembly ever seen in the nation's capital. On August 28, some 250,000 civil-rights activists, led by Martin Luther King, Jr., converged on the Lincoln Memorial to demand full civil rights for blacks. "Jobs and freedom" was the cry of the marchers, including 50,000 whites. They were addressed by a phalanx of supporters including labor

Left: In an attempt to disperse the 3,000-strong crowd protesting segregation, riot police in Birmingham brought out the fire hoses. The force of the spray was strong enough to tear off clothes. Here, three demonstrators join hands against the force of the jet.

leader Walter Reuther, clergymen of many faiths, folk singer Joan Baez, and gospel singer Mahalia Jackson. The unforgettable closing address was delivered by Dr. King, who would receive the Nobel Prize for Peace the following year. At the urging of Mahalia Jackson, who called out from the dais, "Tell them about your dream, Martin! Tell them about the dream!" he put aside his prepared text and moved the immense crowd to tears and exaltation with the words:

I have a dream that one day this nation will rise up and live out the true meaning of its creed: "We hold these truths to be self-evident—that all men are created equal." I have a dream that one day on the red hills of Georgia the sons of former slaves and the sons of former slaveowners will be able to sit down together at the table of brotherhood. I have a dream that one day even the state of Mississippi, a desert state sweltering with the heat of injustice and oppression, will be transformed into an oasis of freedom and justice. I have a dream that my four little children will one day live in a nation where they will not be judged by the color of their skin but by the content of their character.

I have a dream today....

When we let freedom ring, when we let it ring from every village and every hamlet, from every state and every city, we will be able to speed up that day when all of God's children, black men and white men, Jews and Gentiles, Protestants and Catholics, will be able to join hands and sing in the words of the old Negro spiritual, "Free at last! Free at last! Thank God almighty, we are free at last!"

The March on Washington was followed three weeks later by the bombing of Birmingham's Sixteenth Street Baptist Church, in which four children were killed and twenty other persons injured. Clearly the struggle was not over yet. But not even the national tragedy of President Kennedy's assassination that November could dim the light generated by the year's achievements and the growing national consensus on behalf of what A. Philip Randolph had called "a massive moral revolution."

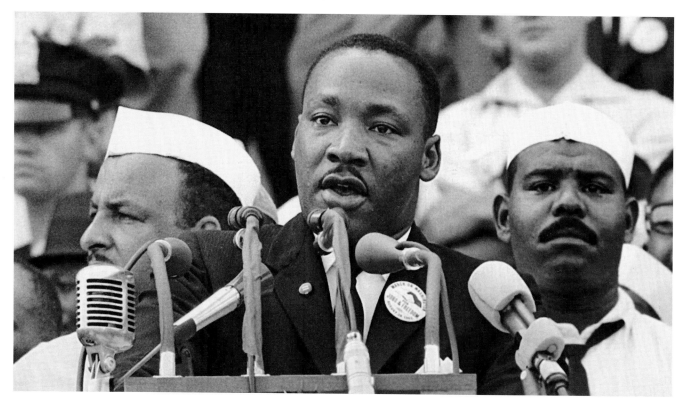

Right: John Lewis, chairman of the SNCC, addresses the crowd from the Lincoln Memorial platform.

Opposite, above: A few of the more than 250,000 men, women, and children who participated in the March on Washington listen raptly to the civil right leaders, clergymen, and other speakers.

Right: Participants in the march hold signs documenting some of their many demands for equal treatment: decent housing, an end to police brutality, integrated schools, and a higher minimum wage.

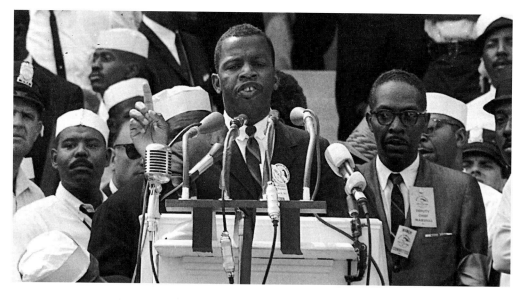

Below: Participants arriving by train from western Pennsylvania. The march attracted individuals and groups from across the country.

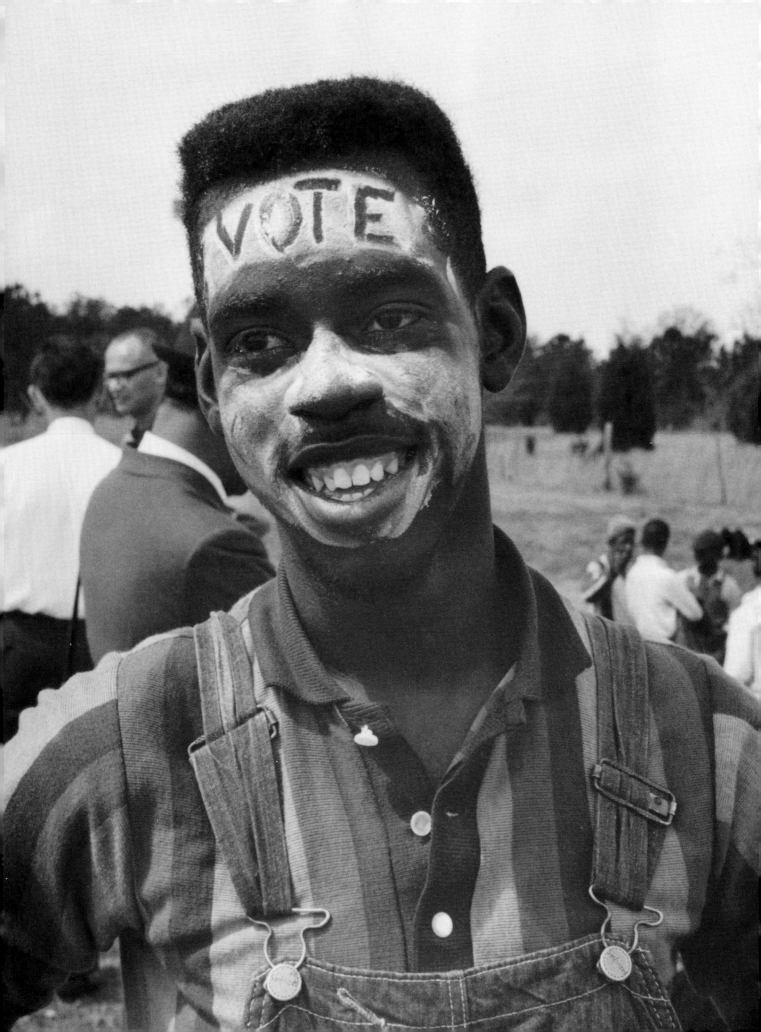

Freedom Summer

"All over the world, like a fever, the freedom movement is spreading in the widest liberation in history."

—MARTIN LUTHER KING, JR., 1964

fter Vice-President Lyndon B. Johnson was inaugurated as Kennedy's successor, his lackluster efforts on behalf of civil rights were replaced by a genuine commitment. He insisted that the strong Civil Rights bill initiated by Kennedy be passed rapidly and without compromise of its provisions. Two days after he gave this message to Congress, he met with NAACP leader Roy Wilkins, then spent the early months of 1964 promoting the civil rights bill on every possible occasion. The Southern bloc had killed such measures before by filibuster, but the shrewd and forceful Johnson, himself a Southerner, was just the man to forestall such tactics. The bill moved forward rapidly in the House of Representatives, while the Senate sought to talk it to death as "a mixed breed of unconstitutionality and the NAACP." Thanks largely to a civil-rights federation formed fifteen years earlier—the Leadership Conference on Civil Rights—a hundred lobbying groups contributed to passage of the measure in July. Would it be enforceable?

Opposite: An affirmation of a U.S. citizen's constitutional right, and an exhortation to exercise it.

Left: NAACP leader Roy Wilkins points out that it has been a year since President Kennedy sent the Civil Rights bill to Congress, a move that Wilkins described as "a giant step" forward.

131

THE CIVIL RIGHTS ACT OF 1964

Passage of the strongest civil rights act in American history to that date resulted from years of effort on the part of black leaders and white supporters. The older organizations, including the NAACP and the Urban League, led by Whitney M. Young, Jr., had focused their efforts on court cases and educational programs. Newer organizations had led the more active forms of protest: the SCLC, CORE, and the SNCC. Black spokes-men and leaders in other spheres had also influenced the victory, including writer James Baldwin, entertainer Dick Gregory, and a host of others. The measures included in the Civil Rights Act of 1964 provided for enforcing equal rights for blacks in the fields of voting, public accommodations, public facilities, education, programs receiving federal aid, and employment. Even diehard opponents like Georgia senator Richard Russell returned to their constituents to urge compliance. In

The Ripple Effect

Long before—and after—the Civil Rights Act of 1964 put federal power behind their efforts to integrate public facilities nationwide, individuals and groups were making courageous efforts to cross the color line. In 1958 nineteen-year-old David Isom (bottom) of St. Petersburg, Florida, took the plunge at one of his city's segregated pools, resulting in its closing by public officials. Six years later, the manager of a motor lodge in St. Augustine, Florida, poured muriatic acid into his pool during this integration protest (left).

Below, LaMar McCoy and three other CORE members appeared at the Muehlebach Hotel's barbershop in Kansas City, Missouri, for haircuts shortly after the first black patron had been accommodated. It was through thousands of such acts of bravery that the walls of discrimination were gradually chipped away.

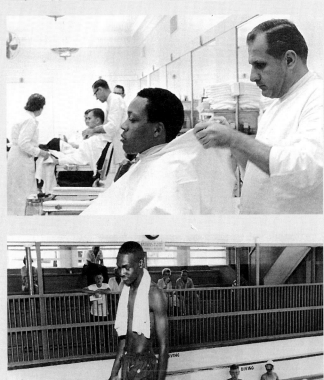

Russell's words, "It is the law of the Senate and we must abide by it." He exhorted Georgians "to refrain from violence in dealing with this act." The previous months' activities had mobilized so much support for the measure that Russell complained privately that he was surrounded on every side by labor spokesmen, women's groups, fraternal and civic organizations, and ministers praying for his enlightenment.

BACK TO MISSISSIPPI

While debate went on in the Halls of Congress during the first few months of 1964, members of the Student Nonviolent Coordinating Committee planned a new offensive: political organization of blacks in the nation's poorest and most bigoted state. Blacks comprised 45 percent of Mississippi's population—the highest of any state—but the caste system that had replaced slavery was almost intact. Black sharecroppers worked white-owned cotton fields for about fifty cents a day. The state constitution of 1890 had been written specifically to disenfranchise black voters, and efforts to vote were commonly countered by beatings, lynchings, and mysterious disappearances.

SNCC workers had first attempted to penetrate rural Mississippi in 1961, under the leadership of Bob Moses, a black graduate student at Harvard. Violent harassment undermined their efforts, but unexpected encouragement had come from Attorney General Robert Kennedy, who implied that movement efforts on behalf of voter registration by civil-rights groups would have federal and private financial support. By April 1962, SNCC and other groups had formed the Voter Education Project, the bulk of its funds directed toward the Magnolia State. A sardonic joke of the period posed the question: "What has four eyes and can't see?" The answer: "Mississippi."

The year 1963 had seen some important gains. Some 80,000 newly registered black voters cast their ballots for Freedom Party delegates in alternate elections to the state Democratic primaries. These ballots went uncounted by white electoral boards, but they represented a moral victory. Moses then planned the "Freedom Summer" project of 1964, whereby black and white student activists would enter every black neighborhood to encourage registration and Freedom Party votes. The effort would be coordinated by the newly formed Council of Federated Organizations (COFO).

Some 900 volunteers were recruited, most of them white students from Ivy League

schools whose social concerns also embraced the nation's growing involvement in Vietnam. King's colleague Andrew Young and other longtime activists tried to warn SNCC that they were risking their lives with little chance of making headway, and President Johnson, alarmed by the prospect of Democratic disunity and potential violence, warned that he could not provide protection for the volunteers.

Mississippi officials mobilized as if for war, doubling the Jackson police force and the highway patrol. Weapons including shotguns and submachine guns were issued, and a bill was enacted "to restrain movements of individuals under certain circumstances." SNCC student recruiter Stokely Carmichael met open opposition from black parents who feared for their childrens' lives, with good reason.

On June 21, a black church in the town of Philadelphia was set on fire even as carloads of volunteers reached the state. Three young workers from the COFO office in Meridian set out to investigate the arson: Michael Schwerner, a twenty-four-year-old Jewish social worker; James Chaney, a nineteen-year-old black native of Meridian; and Andrew Goodman, a twenty-year-old white Freedom Summer worker from New York City. They did not return, and fellow workers feared the worst. Not until early August were their bodies found near a dam in Philadelphia. Schwerner and Goodman had been shot through the head, Chaney had been shot and beaten so savagely that the pathologist reported he had "never witnessed bones so severely shattered" in twenty-five years' experience. The town's deputy sheriff had conspired in their murder before he released them from jail. At least three other civil rights workers would die by violence before the summer ended. In total, the workers experienced a thousand arrests; thirty bombings of homes, churches, and other buildings; eighty

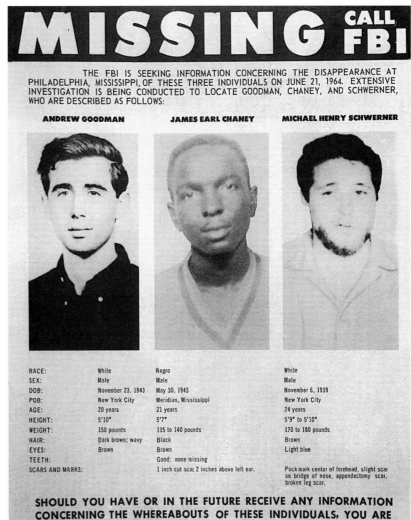

MISSING CALL FBI

THE FBI IS SEEKING INFORMATION CONCERNING THE DISAPPEARANCE AT PHILADELPHIA, MISSISSIPPI, OF THESE THREE INDIVIDUALS ON JUNE 21, 1964. EXTENSIVE INVESTIGATION IS BEING CONDUCTED TO LOCATE GOODMAN, CHANEY, AND SCHWERNER, WHO ARE DESCRIBED AS FOLLOWS:

ANDREW GOODMAN **JAMES EARL CHANEY** **MICHAEL HENRY SCHWERNER**

	ANDREW GOODMAN	JAMES EARL CHANEY	MICHAEL HENRY SCHWERNER
RACE:	White	Negro	White
SEX:	Male	Male	Male
DOB:	November 23, 1943	May 30, 1943	November 6, 1939
POB:	New York City	Meridian, Mississippi	New York City
AGE:	20 years	21 years	24 years
HEIGHT:	5'10"	5'7"	5'9" to 5'10"
WEIGHT:	150 pounds	135 to 140 pounds	170 to 180 pounds
HAIR:	Dark brown; wavy	Black	Brown
EYES:	Brown	Brown	Light blue
TEETH:		Good; none missing	
SCARS AND MARKS:		1 inch cut scar 2 inches above left ear.	Pock mark center of forehead, slight scar on bridge of nose, appendectomy scar, broken leg scar.

SHOULD YOU HAVE OR IN THE FUTURE RECEIVE ANY INFORMATION CONCERNING THE WHEREABOUTS OF THESE INDIVIDUALS, YOU ARE REQUESTED TO NOTIFY ME OR THE NEAREST OFFICE OF THE FBI. TELEPHONE NUMBER IS LISTED BELOW.

beatings; and thirty-five shooting incidents. Their achievements included thousands of new voter registrations, adult literacy classes, "freedom schools" for more than 2,500 children at 41 locations, and the strengthening of grass-roots political activism and leadership among state residents.

THE MOVEMENT IN SELMA

The following year saw passage of the Voting Rights Act of 1965, increasing focus on civil-rights issues by the media, and growing dissension within the movement as Black Power became a force on the national scene (see chapter 9). In January 1965, Dr. King announced that he would call for demonstrations in Alabama if blacks were restrained from registering and voting. Local registrars, in a reprise of the Grandfather Clause, had so complicated the registration process as to deny the ballot to blacks, a process comparable to that in Mississippi. In fact, by 1964 only 2,000,000 of the South's 5,000,000 blacks of voting age had been registered. Judicial attempts to enforce voting rights had proved costly and largely ineffective.

Selma, Alabama, some fifty miles west of the state capital at Montgomery, had a black majority (29,000 inhabitants), of whom only 3 percent were registered to vote. SNCC had laid the groundwork for civil-rights progress there since 1963, against the efforts of Sheriff Jim Clark and his armed and deputized supporters in Dallas County. When Dr. King arrived in January 1965, he was assaulted at the Hotel Albert, where he became the first black person to take a room. His assailant was arrested—Mayor Joseph Smitherman feared bad publicity—and King's committee met to plan strategy.

Next morning, January 20, sixty-seven blacks on their way to the Selma courthouse to register were arrested by Clark for "unlawful assembly." Later in the day, fifty more were

Above: James Farmer (center) joins the silent vigil held in memory of the three victims.

Right: The grieving mothers of Chaney, Goodman, and Schwerner are escorted from their sons' funeral service.

taken into custody. When some 100 black teachers formed a ring of silent protest around the courthouse on January 22, they were driven off with clubs and electric cattle prods. Clark attacked a black woman who defied him three days later—after a federal court order against impeding the registration process—and clubbed her in full view of reporters. National outrage ensued.

On February 1, Drs. King and Abernathy were arrested with more than 700 other demonstrators, most of them children. King directed the protest from jail and aroused national sympathy for the cause with a letter to the American people that said in part "There are more Negroes in jail with me than there are on the voting rolls" (3,000 by this time). Sympathy demonstrations were held in several cities, and SNCC organizers invited

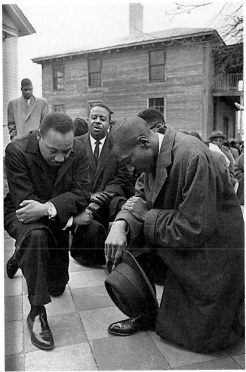

Above: Would-be voters line up to register at the Dallas County Courthouse.

Left: Shortly before the mass arrest of the more than 700 demonstrators, Dr. King kneels to pray on the sidewalk in front of the Selma courthouse.

Political Progress During the 1960s

Hand-in-hand with direct protest by civil-rights activists, the ballot box provided the means for considerable progress during the 1960s. Voter registration, as shown in these scenes in Somerville, Tennessee (right, 1960) and Peachtree, Alabama (below, 1966), forced politicians to pay attention to civil-rights demands.

Newly elected president John F. Kennedy named Andrew Hatcher to serve as press secretary for his administration. In 1961 Robert Weaver became administrator of the Housing and Home Finance Agency, the highest federal post held to that date by an African American. Adam Clayton Powell was elected chairman of the House Education and Labor Committee; James B. Parsons became the first black appointed to a federal district court; and Thurgood Marshall was appointed to the U.S. Circuit Court of Appeals. In 1961 Edward W. Brooke, III, became the first black attorney general of Massachusetts. Born in Washington D.C. on October 26, 1919, Brooke would become the first black elected to the U.S. Senate since Reconstruction, in 1966.

Opposite, congressional candidates Annie Devine, Fannie Lou Hamer, and Victoria Grey were photographed in Washington in January 1965, running for office with the Mississippi Freedom Democratic Party.

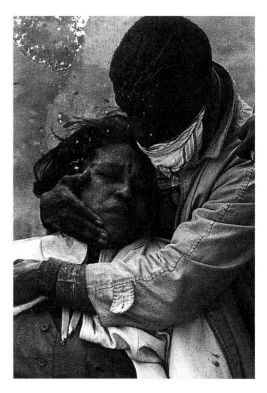

Right: Covering his face with a handkerchief to protect himself from tear gas, a young man cradles a victim of the Selma police in January 1965.

Black Muslim leader Malcolm X to address a Selma church rally on August 3. Nonviolent leaders held their breath, as Malcolm X declared, "The white man should thank God that Dr. King is holding his people in check, because...there are other ways to obtain their ends." Afterward, he conferred with Coretta Scott King and expressed his wish that he could visit her husband in jail.

After additional brutality toward protestors, Sheriff Clark was hospitalized with chest pains in mid-February. He sneered at the prayer vigil conducted for him by the protestors, but one of the black children involved assured inquirers that "We didn't joke with the Lord." Another child observed that demonstrating "just wasn't the same without Jim Clark fussing and fuming."

THE MARCH TO MONTGOMERY

On March 7, some 600 demonstrators, led by John Lewis of SNCC and organizer Hosea Williams, undertook a planned five-day march from Selma to the state capital at Montgomery. This initial attempt was stopped by 200 state troopers and possemen from the Dallas County Sheriff's Office,

wielding tear gas, nightsticks, and whips. The rationale for this and the ensuing riot in the black quarter by Clark's men was that the march had been banned by Governor George Wallace. The attempt to cross the Edmund Pettus Bridge across the Alabama River ended in the assault that was known as "Bloody Sunday." State troopers on horseback clubbed demonstrators as dense clouds of tear gas rose over the scene. Andrew Young would recall, "The tear gas was so thick you couldn't get to where the people were who needed help." Marchers retreated to Brown's Chapel, their starting point, and Dr. King—who had been sent to Atlanta for his safety after death threats—called for a nationwide ministers' march to Montgomery on March 9. The injured John Lewis announced: "I don't see how President Johnson can send troops to Vietnam...and can't send troops to Selma, Alabama." It took the intervention of federal judge Frank M. Johnson, Jr., and a second failed attempt to march, to prevail upon Governor Wallace and other state officials to let the demonstration begin on March 21.

Below: Dr. King leads several thousand demonstrators in their long-awaited march from Selma to Montgomery. This successful attempt began on March 21, following two thwarted marches on the seventh and ninth.

By the time the march stepped off from Browns Chapel to the Edmund Pettus Bridge, its ranks had swelled from some five hundred to several thousand. President Johnson had summoned Governor George Wallace to the White House and warned him that state and local authorities must protect the marchers or he would send in federal troops. Black and white supporters from across the country had responded to King's call, and many clergymen were present, including Rabbi Abraham Heschel and the tireless Dr. Ralph Abernathy, who summed up the spirit of the day when he proclaimed, "Wallace, it's all over now." Dr. King and his wife, Coretta, led off with John Lewis and other aides, while Andrew Young was everywhere at once, encouraging the tired, the sunburned, and the young people, whose elders praised them warmly. "These kids are the great ones," Foster and Amelia Boynton told a white onlooker. "They were ahead of their parents and their teachers."

Four days after leaving for Montgomery, the mud-spattered coalition, including the seventy-eight-year-old grandfather of young Jimmy Lee Jackson, who had been shot to death in Selma, finally reached the capital. March 25 saw the greatest assemblage for civil rights since the March on Washington. Dr. King and Coretta King were joined on the speakers' platform by Ralph Abernathy, John Lewis, Roy Wilkins, Whitney Young, A. Philip Randolph, Bayard Rustin, and United Nations diplomat Ralph Bunche.

As before, violence marred the celebration. Four Klansmen shot march participant Viola Liuzzo of Detroit on Highway 80 that night as she returned to the capital after driving marchers back to Selma. Shortly thereafter, members of the Student Nonviolent Coordinating Committee broke with traditional leadership and took a separatist stance on the philosophy of black consciousness. Northern white activists were expelled, and

the young Stokely Carmichael assumed leadership from John Lewis. The emphasis was on political power, third parties, self-determination, and black studies. In 1966 Carmichael was succeeded by H. Rap Brown. By the time of Dr. King's assassination in Memphis, on April 4, 1968, during a meeting with activists Jesse Jackson and Ralph Abernathy, the movement had entered a new phase. As *Eyes on the Prize* author Juan Williams concludes: "[Its] emphasis shifted from the moral imperatives that had garnered support from the nation's moderates—issues such as the right to vote and the right to a decent education—to issues whose moral rightness was not as readily apparent: job and housing discrimination, Johnson's war on poverty, and affirmative action.... Nonviolence was no longer the only tool for change...But the violent events of later years and the many new directions of the civil rights movement cannot obscure the remarkable accomplishments wrought by the men and women, black and white, who in ten short years rewove the fabric of American society."

Above: Waving American flags to emphasize their rights as citizens, civil rights demonstrators converge on the state capitol of Montgomery, Alabama, victoriously completing their protest march from Selma.

The Passing of a Prophet

Like prophets before him, Martin Luther King, Jr., had foreseen the manner of his death. On April 3, 1968, he told an assembly in Memphis, Tennessee, that he was certain of the triumph of racial justice. "I may not get there with you," he predicted, "but...we as a people will get to the promised land."

The following day, as he stood on his motel balcony with Dr. Abernathy and Jesse Jackson, an assassin's bullet from a high-powered rifle shattered his jaw and left him dying.

Tens of thousands followed the mule-drawn caisson (opposite) bearing King's body to his funeral at Atlanta's Ebenezer Baptist Church on April 9 (below). Of the many tributes, written and spoken, one of the most eloquent came from Robert F. Kennedy, who would soon be cut down by an assassin's gun himself:

"Considering the evidence...[that white people] were responsible, you can be filled with bitterness and with hatred and a desire for revenge...Or we can make an effort, as Martin Luther King did, to understand and to comprehend and replace that violence, that stain of bloodshed that has spread across our land, with an effort to understand, compassion and love."

New Leaders, New Agendas

"I am neither a fanatic nor a dreamer. I am a Black man who loves peace and justice and loves his people."

—MALCOLM X, 1965

During the mid-1960s, the Black Power movement became a major influence, primarily among Northern blacks. Its best-known exponent was the brilliant Malcolm X (born Malcolm Little), leader of the Black Muslims/Nation of Islam, founded in Detroit by Elijah (Poole) Muhammed during the 1930s. By 1965 Malcolm X had become a charismatic speaker, urging blacks to end oppression "by any means necessary." Black Power leaders in Northern venues urged separation rather than integration and raised black pride and self-awareness with the affirmation "Black Is Beautiful." They saw institutionalized racism as "The Enemy" rather than individual bigots, and they had little confidence in the non-violent tactics of leaders who sought to achieve equality by doing away with discriminatory laws (although they sometimes formed an uneasy alliance with them). The difference between the two movements is clear in the way Black Power proponents viewed the 1956 attempt to integrate the University of Alabama. To them, the issue was not simply whether black students were admitted. What mattered equally was what that university, and others, were teaching.

NEW LEADERS

Malcolm X, born in Omaha, Nebraska, in 1925, had a troubled youth after the death of his father in 1931: the family believed he had been murdered for his support of Marcus Garvey's ideas. Malcolm became involved with the Harlem underworld during his teens and spent five years in prison for burglary. He educated himself and joined the Nation of Islam while incarcerated. Released in 1952, he became an energetic recruiter and powerful spokesman for the movement, which advocated black nationalism and economic self-sufficiency. He was instrumental in setting up a series of mosques where worshippers reclaimed their heritage of dignity and favor in the eyes of Allah through a racial interpretation of Islam. Within a few years, the Muslims had developed successful farming operations in several

Opposite: Members of the Black Panther Party, a militant organization that urged African Americans to arm themselves against their oppressors, march to a news conference at the United Nations Plaza in New York City in 1968 to protest the imprisonment of the party's cofounder, Huey P. Newton.

Left: Black Muslim spokesman Malcolm X, one of the strongest advocates for black nationalism, speaks in support of the desegregation protestors in Birmingham, Alabama, in May 1963.

Above: After resigning from the Black Muslim movement, Malcolm X prophesied that 1964 would be "the bloodiest year yet in the civil rights fight."

Right: As Malcolm X's body is carried from the funeral service at Faith Temple, New York City, distraught supporters reach out in a gesture of farewell.

states and businesses ranging from clothing stores to real estate to the most widely read black newspaper in the nation. Dissension within the Muslim ranks led to Malcolm X's expulsion in 1963, followed by his pilgrimage to Mecca. There he took the name El-Hajj Malik El-Shabazz and returned to the United States to found the Organization for Afro-American Unity. Malcolm X was assassinated by three disaffected Muslims at a Harlem rally on February 21, 1965, only eighteen days after he spoke in Selma, Alabama, on behalf of the civil rights demonstration there. He was thirty-nine years old.

Bobby Seale and Huey P. Newton were the founders of the Black Panther Party for Self-Defense (1966), in which militant Eldridge Cleaver played a prominent role until he sought political asylum in Algeria. The Black Panthers refused to cooperate with "the decadent, reactionary, racist system" that they perceived as intractable. They organized their own community-based projects, including free breakfasts for ghetto children, health clinics and testing for sickle-cell anemia (contracted mainly by blacks) and food distribution centers. Frequent confrontations with the police ended in death or imprisonment for many members: many of those who survived eventually repudiated the militant posture that had

expressed their frustration and anger.

Stokely Carmichael had adopted the phrase "Black Power" from Congressman Adam Clayton Powell of New York City, who first used the term in the 1950s in a nonviolent context. After his expulsion from the SNCC, Carmichael continued his political activism with the Black Panthers. His successor at SNCC, H. Rap Brown, was jailed on charges of riot and arson in 1970.

BATTLEGROUNDS

Non-Southern cities were the scene of race riots fueled by long-standing frustration, beginning with the 1964 riot in Harlem, followed by the Watts eruption in Los Angeles in 1965. In both cases high unemployment and police brutality against African Americans were the sparks that set off the conflagration. Thirty-five people were killed in the Watts riot, more than 800 were arrested, and property damage totaled more than two-hundred million dollars.

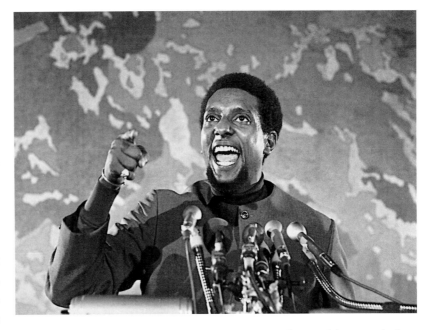

These "long hot summers" were followed by major riots in Chicago and Cleveland (1966), Newark and Detroit (1967), and Washington, D.C., and Cleveland (1968). The commission appointed by President Lyndon B. Johnson to investigate the causes of the riots identified "white racism" as the primary

Above: Stokely Carmichael led the SNCC toward a separatist, more militant stance.

Left: A convoy of National Guard trucks enters the Watts district in Los Angeles during the 1965 riots. Before calm was re-established, thirty-five people had been killed and over eight hundred arrested.

Pride

Beginning in the 1960s, African-American leaders raised ethnic consciousness with such positive slogans as "Black is beautiful." Black Americans increasingly celebrated their ethnic and cultural heritage as distinct and valuable. "Afro" hairstyles, as worn by these Black Panthers (left), became popular. Children learned that they were a source of pride to the community and that their aspirations and ambitions could be fulfilled (below). Olympic medalists Tommie Smith and John Carlos electrified the crowd at the 1968 games in Mexico City when they gave the Black Power salute during the awards ceremony (opposite). New possibilities were everywhere.

Right: Protestors gather outside Madison Square Garden on October 24, 1968, during a rally for presidential candidate George C. Wallace.

problem (Kerner Commission's "Report on Civil Disorders," 1968). Contributing factors cited were unemployment, inadequate housing, and discriminatory police practices. Most of these causes were related to *de facto* rather than *de jure* segregation. SNCC leader H. Rap Brown, still in his twenties, was both applauded and vilified when he said in the wake of urban riots, "Burn, baby, burn!" After he replaced Carmichael as head of SNCC, the organization changed its name to Student National Coordinating Committee (1969). Its policies became increasingly controversial, and it faded from the public scene during the 1970s.

DR. KING'S LEGACY

Dr. Ralph Abernathy assumed leadership of the Southern Christian Leadership Conference in the wake of Dr. King's assassination in April 1968. Since late 1967, the group had been shifting its focus to encompass a broader agenda than straightforward desegregation issues: Dr.

King and some of his colleagues became outspoken critics of the U.S. involvement in Vietnam, and the SCLC began to concentrate on economic issues and the formation of coalitions with other groups disproportion-

Below: Exhausted soldiers welcome the chance to sleep wherever they can find it after the Washington, D.C., riots in the wake of Dr. King's assassination (April 1968).

Left: CORE leaders including new national director Roy Innis (second from right) outline a new national statement of purpose at this September 1968 meeting.

ately affected by poverty, including Hispanics and Native Americans. The first widespread demonstration arising from the antipoverty effort was the Poor People's Campaign of May-June 1968, a protest that had originated with Dr. King. Following his assassination, colleagues including Abernathy, Hosea Williams, and James Bevel resolved to continue with the plans for a high-profile nationwide demonstration, in which the poor and dispossessed would assemble in full view of politicians and the media at the height of the presidential election campaign.

Unfortunately, the uneasy alliance that converged on Washington, D.C., to build the shanty town optimistically called "Resurrection City" did not prove enduring. Bayard Rustin soon withdrew his reluctant support—he had opposed the idea on the grounds that violence was only too likely. Most demonstrators cooperated peacefully in the ambitious construction and running of Resurrection City—whose "mayor" was Jesse Jackson—but there were incidents of robbery, assault, even rape that demeaned the Poor People's Campaign in the public eye,

and city officials, who had dealt with widespread violence and property damage in the riots following King's murder, were in no mood to countenance further trouble.

In the presidential race, African-American leaders and voters put their hopes in the late-blooming candidacy of Robert Kennedy, the only national figure who seemed capable of preventing the forces of polarization from blocking further real progress on civil rights. Candidates for the Republican nomination, including Ronald Reagan, stressed tough law-and-order policies to combat the urban civil unrest. On June 5, after a major primary victory in California, Kennedy was assassinated. His funeral cortège, en route to Arlington Cemetery, stopped at Resurrection City, where the demoralized protestors, still reeling from the loss of Dr. King, paid their final respects. After heavy rains flooded the shanty town, the ill-fated Poor People's Campaign collapsed at the end of June with the arrest of the remaining demonstrators. Richard Nixon's subsequent election victory heralded a national agenda that would place civil rights issues at a low priority.

CONTRASTS AND COMMON CAUSE

Despite their vast differences in tactics and styles of dissent, African-American leaders were increasingly determined to find a platform through which to unite in expressing pride in their ethnic and cultural heritage and to determine how best to pursue their social and political goals. At the 1972 Gary Convention, Coretta Scott King shared the podium with Black Panther Bobby Seale. The convention addressed issues ranging from unemployment to child welfare. That same year, United Church of Christ minister Benjamin Chavis, future head of the NAACP, was arrested in Wilmington, North Carolina, with nine others in a case arising from a protest by high school students. He would serve more than four years in prison.

Black Catholics became more visible on the religious and political scene from 1968, when their bishops issued a call for all Roman Catholics to take a firm stand against racism in housing, education, and employment. African-American college students made their presence felt on campuses across the nation with demands for black studies, open admission, and sometimes separate quarters. Having turned away from cooperation with white students during the late 1960s, they renewed ties with them during the 70s to protest the Vietnam War.

Since the 1970s, both major gains and major setbacks have marked the progress of civil rights in the United States. Discrimination remains in education, employment, and housing, despite the substantial changes effected by affirmative-action programs. Racial tension continues to erupt in various contexts, from the 1994 Los Angeles riots to the rash of attacks on Southern churches in 1996. The goal of full equality that has motivated activists since the era of slavery is not yet a reality. But nothing can undo what was achieved during the 1950s and '60s, when the Civil Rights Movement became a trajectory that flashed across the sky of the nation and the world to illuminate the power of active nonviolence in the cause of justice and freedom.

Right: The NAACP continues its campaign for voter registration in this August 1984 demonstration.

Afterword: My Personal Journey to Awareness

As Civil Rights demonstrations took place across the country, there were blacks in small towns like mine who had no opportunity for direct involvement. During the period that Dr. King was in Albany, Georgia, rumors circulated that Waycross had been targeted as the next town, but no such activity materialized.

On another occasion, we students were told to come to a mass meeting at a church near our high school. Word spread that we would discuss a school walk-out to protest our deteriorating and under-equipped high school and demand that city officials build us new facilities. The school was threatened with losing its accreditation with the State Board of Higher Education if improvements were not made. Parents with the funds to send their children to college were anxious about this and backed the idea of a walk-out. But plans went awry. Instead of the big-time political rally we had anticipated, much to our chagrin, our high school principal stood nervously before us with the threat to suspend anyone who participated in a school boycott. If not for the media and a few courageous teachers and preachers, who dared to speak from where they stood, we might never have known a race revolution was occurring in America.

From television we learned of bombings, lynchings, marches, and sit-ins—stories that were expanded in black publications like *Jet, Ebony,* and the *Pittsburgh Courier.* In addition to recording our political victories and defeats, these black publications highlighted our social accomplishments, thereby inspiring the less fortunate to believe that they, too, could accomplish great things and rise above their circumstances.

For me, literature also played a pivotal part in my maturation. As I read Langston Hughes, Richard Wright, and Frank Yerby (the few black authors available in my segregated hometown library) I knew there was something better for me than what I had experienced in Waycross, Georgia.

In 1963, the year I graduated from high school, I still earned fifty cents per hour for performing domestic work on weekends and child care after school. From seventh grade on, I had worked as a babysitter for a medical doctor and his wife who had five children under the age of

ten. Exhausted from the job, I counted the days until I would be able to escape. While I was not forced to work by my parents, I wanted income of my own, and this was the only kind of job the average black teenage girl could secure in the South during the 1950s and early '60s. There was an occasional dishwasher/short-order cook job, but most of these positions went to adults, who considered them good jobs. There were, of course, the cotton and tobacco fields and warehouses where teenagers could find employment, but health reasons prevented me from doing this kind of work. Many of my friends worked in the tobacco fields and warehouses, but few picked cotton. Those who worked in the tobacco warehouses said that it was suffocating and back-breaking labor. The King Edward Cigar Factory was a major business in my hometown. Originally, it had closed its doors to Negroes—until many whites became seriously ill from working in the improperly ventilated factory. Those blacks who were finally hired saw this as a good opportunity, despite the health risks. One adult I knew worked at the King Edward factory during the week and as a beautician on weekends. She shared with me on a trip home that years after she stopped working in the cigar factory, the smell of tobacco still came from her perspiration.

Whether they were cropping or sorting and grading tobacco, I felt that my friends' tasks were no more laborious than my domestic work. Many a Saturday, as I moved from room to room of the white woman's house, cleaning, doing laundry, and chasing after children, I would dream of the day my change would come. Had there been no end in sight, I would have had to quit this job before completing high school.

Upon graduating from my segregated high school in 1963, I left the South to join Northern relatives, in my case, an older sister who had made the journey to "the promised land." While living with our aunt, my sister had completed a nursing degree program and married. In the black tradition, it was now her turn to guide me on my way. And the cycle would continue as I helped the next sibling in the family.

In the cases of outstanding students whose families were too poor to send them either to college or to a relative, local black teachers and the community at large would find ways to come to their aid. Their efforts gave meaning to the expression "A mind is a terrible thing to waste" long before it was popularized by the United Negro College Fund. These gestures of generosity came without fanfare; the donors sometimes remained anonymous. I was out of high school before I learned that my elementary school principal had given financial assistance to many students in our town. This same woman (like other teachers I knew in the South) willed large sums of money to black scholarship funds and institutions of higher learning.

Another passage of escape from the segregated South for young women was through "sleep-in" jobs. White women advertised for young women to come North at their expense and live in their homes as housekeepers and child-care providers. Black high school seniors responded to these ads, traveling by Greyhound or Trailways buses, the cheapest means of transportation. As tiring as the long, lonesome rides North were, desperation to leave the South prompted many young women to accept these tickets to unknown futures. Since they had always been warned against going off with white strangers, it was baffling that parents accepted this as a risk worth taking. But those who remained behind needed the financial assistance sent back from daughters up North.

The "sleep-in girls" (as they were called) often ended up in isolated areas of Long Island, where they worked around the clock, rising early to take care of children, cooking, cleaning, washing, and ironing. The object of their having a room in the house was their availability to answer the nighttime cries of other women's children.

On Thursdays and every-other-weekends off, the young women frequented small clubs and taverns on Long Island where other transplanted Southerners socialized. In time, they would venture into New York City and discover such regional bars as the Peachtree in Harlem, where blacks from Georgia congregated, and the Tar Heel Lounge in Brooklyn, where North Carolinians gathered.

But the church was the primary sustainer of young girls from the South. Here they met older women who had been the route and were eager to take them under their wings. The local church I attended in Harlem had several young women who had come up from Mississippi. The church ladies not only helped liberate them from their sleep-in jobs, but served as matchmakers in marrying them off to eligible bachelors in the congregation.

The Young Women's Christian Association (YWCA) and the YMCA were also havens for young people in transit. When church women directed the sleep-in-girls to other jobs, the "Y" was often the place they stayed until they saved enough to rent an apartment. Some church women rented rooms in their homes. I was fortunate enough not only to get such a room, but to have a kitchen and bathroom that I shared with only one adjoining tenant. Because of a change in my brother-in-law's job, my sister was forced to leave New York shortly after I arrived. Panic set in as I considered my future. My sister invited me to join her and her husband in Boston, but this was not my choice. Nor did I want to consider moving in with my aunt, whom she had lived with under strict rules. I wanted to be on my own, but knew that this was not likely on the $63.00 a week I now made as a bank clerk. So rooming with a church family became my only other alternative. Because I was a rent-paying tenant, I thought there would be total independence, but soon discovered that the church lady was as strict on me as my aunt would have been. I had to attend church every Sunday, just as I did growing up in Georgia. She used the tactic of calling me to join them downstairs for breakfast. We not only attended church every week, but Sunday School as well!

My landlady had a daughter my age with whom I socialized. One Saturday night, at a club she had taken me to in Greenwich Village, my dance partner asked if I smoked. When I replied "No," he then asked if I drank, to which I had to say "No" again. He then quipped, "And I bet you're going to Sunday School in the morning!" I laughed as though it were a joke, but this was exactly where I would be the next day. No matter how late we stayed out on Saturday evening, we still had to rise and shine on Sunday. While it annoyed me at the time, I realize today that the discipline my landlady instilled helped build character and was a gift passed by black women like her from generation to generation.

Since the church we attended was in Harlem, I got a weekly glimpse of life in the city. But it was in reading Claude Brown's coming-of-age novel *Manchild in the Promised Land* that I came to understand the hardships of inner-city life for the poor. I also saw their living conditions, as I visited the cramped apartments of some members of my church. As poor as I had felt my existence was growing up in the South, it seemed better to me than having to grow up in the air-tight apartments I saw in Harlem. Although we never had enough room in the houses we rented at home, one could at least find refuge on front porches, in backyards, and in the outdoors generally. The littered streets and abandoned lots of the city offered little serenity, as far as I could see.

Church youths invited me to movies, concerts, on boat rides to Bear Mountain, and to a variety of other activities. I thought my social life was dull at the time, but it was good that some-one as naive and unsophisticated as I was during the 1960s fell under the watchful eye of an upright church family.

Attending concerts at the famous Apollo Theatre, I began to see and hear some of the political action that was tak-ing place in the streets. I stared with curiosity, but never had the courage to stop and listen to the street-corner philosophers, or to purchase *Muhammad Speaks,* the Muslim paper sold by neatly dressed young men on almost every corner in Harlem. Malcolm X had broken with the Nation of Islam and collaborated with Alex Haley on the publi-cation of *The Autobiography of Malcolm X,* a book that was a major influence on me.

A national event that raised my political awareness was the Mississippi murder of civil-rights workers James Chaney, Michael Schwerner, and Andrew Goodman, all in their early twenties. As with the murder of Emmett Till in my youth, I was deeply saddened by the death of young per-sons so close to my own age. The fact that two of the vic-tims were white also served as a reminder that hatred and discrimination in the South remained boundless. Mississippi was especially violent. Shortly after the murder of the three young civil-rights activists, two more blacks were killed in Vicksburg, Mississippi, in a church bombing—the church had been used as a voter registration center.

While I knew no one involved in the Black Panther Party or any other revolutionary movement, I felt an affinity with those contemporaries who dared to take on the system. The hopelessness that had brought about the cries of "Black Power" was widespread. I understood and identified with athletes Tommie Smith and John Carlos, whose youthful political idealism made them raise clenched fists in the Black Power salute during the 1968 Olympic games.

There was ever-increasing cause for unrest among black young adults. We had lost another of our emerging heroes with the murder of Malcolm X in New York City, race riots were breaking out on college campuses and in various cities, and unemployment was on the rise. In February 1968, the results of the government-sponsored Kerner Report were published: it predicted that the nation was moving rapidly toward two societies—one black, one white. Recommendations were made to improve urban life. The proposals included federal input into better housing, greater access to education, more employment opportunities, and the enhancement of interracial communication. The latter directive opened the door for schools and libraries to pur-chase more books on black subjects. Subsequently, pub-lishers began seeking new black writers.

Since the church I attended was fundamentalist, there was no participation in politics, despite its being an all-black congregation in a turbulent period vis-á-vis race relations. At a national summer youth conference I took part in, the race issue was raised by a group of young people just out of college. They pressed the leaders to define the church's role in the movement—only to be silenced by the elders for inappropriate comments. This response from the church caused me (and many of my generation) to step back from close involvement, as seen in Carolyn Rodger's poem "It Must Be Deep," an exchange between a college-age daugh-ter and her mother on the daughter's belief in God. While I did not stop attending church or abandon my faith, my passion was not as intense.

In time, I found employment and began attending evening classes at Hunter College. Although political activity was high on college campuses across the country, this did not extend to evening students. Like me, most worked all day and had little energy for anything else beyond their stud-ies. By now I had established many friendships in New York, including those with young men being drafted into the army. The young man I dated volunteered in an effort to have more choices than Vietnam in his place of assignment. His haste in signing up was followed by a quick proposal of marriage so that I could accompany him to his alterna-tive posting, which turned out to be Alaska!

I abandoned job, college, and friends and followed him to the "old" Alaska—a state without the modern conve-niences of today. During our two-year stay, there was one television station with limited hours. I learned of the death of Martin Luther King from a very ignorant and racist Southern woman who lived next door in the trailer camp where we stayed. I had no idea she could be so insensitive as to face me, or any other black person, and say that she had no trouble with colored people, but felt that Martin Luther King was "a big troublemaker who kinda' had it comin'!" The image of that wide-eyed ignorant woman as she shocked me with these words remains vivid to this day. Here was a person whom I had trusted to watch my first-born if I had to do a quick errand, and I had, in turn, watched her infant. Never would I have believed that she was capable of desecrating the memory of someone so noble as Dr. King. It was an eye-opener for me.

Only once before had I needed to reassess my relationship with a white person I thought I knew. The other case had been that of the woman for whom I worked during my high school years. The fact that she never saw fit to raise my pay from fifty cents an hour should have alerted me to the fact that my well-being was not her highest priority. But somehow, I excused her, convincing myself that she had to maintain the status quo by keeping to the rate that every other colored maid (including my mother) was being paid. I never questioned it, or expected to be paid more. My turning point with her came over another matter, but one big enough to count. While driving me home from work one day, she began to trash the Democratic Party and to rave about Barry Goldwater. I was no political animal at seventeen, but I was wise enough to discern who was on my side, and I knew that it wasn't Barry Goldwater! So I decided that perhaps she wasn't either—at least not deep down, as the poet Rodgers suggests. I was not only a laborer, but a confidante, long before a girl my age needed to be burdened with the details of a failing marriage. But in retrospect, having to hear her stories was beneficial in that I learned that spousal abuse was widespread and didn't happen only in black families. Although painful at the time, these attitude shifts toward two white women were significant moments of growth in the development of relationships with persons outside my race.

Upon returning to New York, I re-established my life in the city and gave birth to a second child. The 1970s were essentially child-rearing years for me, but I continued to be an avid reader. The proliferation of black books during this period increased my appetite for reading even more, and the library was my second home. I also delighted in the great number of stories for and about black children. One day I went to the library for books for my youngest daughter, who was perhaps three years old at the time. I let her sit in on a reading session for small children. She happened to be the only black child among the dozen or so present, but I did not see this as a problem. However, as we were leaving, my beautiful little black girl began to cry and said that she was the only one there who was not pretty. As I sought to comfort her, I struggled to understand why she had drawn such a conclusion. I realized that not only had she been the only one of her kind, but all the characters in the story had been blond white children. It was not easy for my little girl that day. This incident highlighted for me the importance of African American children having images of themselves. A lover of words, I committed myself to adding to the body of literature on black life.

I began to create stories and poems about everyday events in the lives of my children and those around them. Crisis in my marriage also led to my writing personal poetry. I learned of a writers' workshop being held at the Countee Cullen Library in Harlem and joined this group. Led by poet and professor Sonia Sanchez (who currently chairs a department at Temple University) the group met every week. While attending the workshop led by Ms. Sanchez, I learned of a second writers' group taught by the late John Oliver Killens at Columbia University. It was under the tutelage of Professors Sanchez and Killens that I learned the craft of writing. Both were strong social activists, so I could not have been in better hands. They not only taught me *how* to write, but helped develop my awareness of the writer's social responsibility.

Editors from Harper and Row (now HarperCollins) heard me recite some of my children's poems during a reading at Countee Cullen and sought me out. My first book, *Ludell,* which they published in 1975, was nominated for a National Book Award in children's literature.

In addition to my desire to create for children, I have begun to reflect in later years that my passion for writing also results from my having being absent from the marches and other civil rights activities that were so close as I came along, yet so far away. Telling the stories is a small contribution. In so doing, I have looked deeply into the question of black roots in America and contemporary developments like affirmative action.

The standard refrain of many white Americans on the question of affirmative action in employment, education, and housing is: "I don't feel that I should pay for the sins of my forefathers." Even those willing to admit the justice of this form of reparation for centuries of discrimination against blacks are beginning to cry "Enough!" The prevailing sentiment is that there has been a sufficient leveling-out period and that the time has come for all citizens to start at the same point: There should be no more "set-asides" or other advantages based on racial considerations.

National debate on the issue of affirmative action is no longer limited to white and black Americans, but has come to include Asians, Hispanics, and other ethnic groups. However, black Americans' leadership role in the Civil Rights Movement, and their unique role as the only group that was brought to this country involuntarily, have placed the major focus of affirmative action between blacks and whites. Professor Lani Guinier, reportedly passed over as a candidate for U.S. Attorney General for her views on affirmative action; Professor Stephen Carter, author of *Reflections of An Affirmative Action Baby*; and Supreme Court justice Clarence Thomas are among the prominent African Americans who have offered opinions on this controversial subject.

Responding to the decision of the Board of Regents of the University of California at Berkeley to end its affirmative action policy, Chancellor Chang Lin-tien stated in a *New York Times* article of March 1996, "America has come a long way since the days of Jim Crow segregation. It would be a tragedy if our nation's colleges and universities slipped backward now, denying access to talented but disadvantaged youth and eroding the diversity that helps to prepare leaders."

As we approach the year 2000, affirmative action is clearly an issue of racial divisiveness. Another and even more disturbing matter of racial discord is that of the rise of hate crimes. Antigovernment militia groups exist in thirty-one states. In 1995–6 more than two dozen black churches across the country were destroyed by fire. So the struggle continues. But as dismal as the picture of race relations may appear, the works of historians including Carter G. Woodson, W.E.B. Du Bois, John Hope Franklin, Vincent Harding, William Loren Katz, and Lerone Bennett give ground for hope. These scholars, who have provided a seminal body of work on African-American history, remind us that there will always be persons of moral suasion dedicated to the cause of social justice.

—*Brenda Wilkinson, 1996*

Bibliography and Works Cited

Bennett, Lerone, Jr. *Before the Mayflower: A History of Black America*, rev. ed. New York: Viking Penguin, 1984.

Bontemps, Arna, *100 Years of Negro Freedom*. New York: Dodd Mead & Co., 1961.

Boyle, Sarah. *The Desegregated Heart*. New York: William Morrow & Co., 1962.

Branch, Taylor. *Parting the Waters: America in the King Years*. New York: Touchstone, 1989.

Carson, Clayborne, ed. *The Movement (1964–1970)*. Compiled by the staff of The Martin Luther King Jr. Papers Project. Westport, CT: Greenwood Press, 1992.

Findlay, James F., Jr. *Church Life in the Struggle: The NCC and the Black Church Movement*. New York: Oxford University Press, 1993.

Franklin, John Hope. *From Slavery to Freedom*. New York: Alfred Knopf, 1948.

Garrow, David. *Bearing the Cross*. New York: William Morrow, 1986.

Hansen, Joyce. *Between Two Fires: Black Soldiers in the Civil War*. New York: Franklin Watts, 1993.

Harding, Vincent. *The Other American Revolution*. Atlanta: Regents of University of California & The Institute of the Black World, 1980.

———. *There is a River: The Black Struggle for Freedom in America*. New York: Harcourt Brace Jovanovich, 1981.

Harley, Sharon. *The Timetables of American History*. New York: Simon & Schuster, 1995.

Haskins, James, and Benson, Kathleen. *The 60's Reader*. New York: Viking Penguin, 1988.

Jackson, James S. *Black Life in America*. Newbury Park: Sage Publications, 1991.

Johnson, Charles S. *Growing Up in the Black Belt: Negro Youth in the Rural South*. Washington, D.C.: American Council on Education, 1941.

Katz, William Loren. *Eyewitness: The Negro in American History; A Living Documentary of the Afro-American Contribution to U.S. History*. Pitman Publishing Corp., 1967.

Long, Richard. *Black America*. Secaucus, NJ: Chartwell Books Inc., 1985.

Morris, Aldon. *Origin of the Civil Rights Movement*. New York: The Free Press, 1984.

Oates, Stephen B. *Let The Trumpet Sound: The Life of Martin Luther King, Jr.* New York: Harper & Row, 1982.

Powledge, Fred. *Free At Last: The Civil Rights Movement and the People Who Made It*. Boston: Little Brown & Co, 1991.

Quarles, Benjamin. *The Negro in the Civil War*. Boston: Little Brown & Co., 1953.

Redding, J. Saunders. *On Being Negro in America*. New York: Bobbs Merrill, 1951.

———. *The Lonesome Road*. New York: Doubleday, 1958.

Report of the National Advisory Commission on Civil Disorder, New York: New York Times Co., 1960

Reynolds, Barbara. *The Movement, The Myth*. Chicago: Nelson-Hill, 1975.

Seymour, Robert. *Whites Only: A Pastor's Retrospective of Signs of the New South*. Valley Forge, PA: Judson Press, 1991.

St. James, Warren. *NAACP*. Smithtown, NY: Exposition Press, 1958.

Washington, James, ed. *A Testament of Hope: The Essential Writings of Martin Luther King, Jr.* San Francisco: Harper & Row, 1989.

West, Cornell. *Race Matters*. Boston: Beacon Press, 1993.

Williams, Juan. *Eyes on the Prize: America's Civil Rights Years, 1954–65*. New York: Viking Penguin, 1981.

Woodson, Carter G . *The Story of the Negro Retold*. Washington, D.C.: The Associated Press, 1935.

———. *The Negro in Our History*. Washington, D.C.: Associated Publishers, 1922.

———. *From Slavery to Freedom: A History of Negro America*. New York: Alfred Knopf, 1980.

———. *The Education of the Negro Prior to 1861*. New York: G.A. Putnam & Sons, 1915.

———. *The History of the Negro Church*. Washington, D.C.: Associated Publishers, 1921.

Index